Family History Cultures and Faiths

Acknowledgements

The publishers would like to
thank Abi Husainy, Records Specialist
at the National Archives, Kew, for her
valuable contribution of chapter 8,
South Asian cultures and faiths,
to this book.

Family History Cultures and Faiths

How your ancestors lived and worshipped

Michael Gandy

the national archives

First published in 2007 by
The National Archives
Kew, Richmond
Surrey, TW9 4DU, UK

www.nationalarchives.gov.uk

The National Archives brings together the Public Record Office,
Historical Manuscripts Commission, Office of Public Sector
Information and Her Majesty's Stationery Office.

ISBN 978 1 905615 11 7

Typeset by Textype, Cambridge, UK
Cover designed by Briony Hartley / Goldust Design
Printed by MPG Books, Bodmin, Cornwall,UK

Contents

Picture Acknowledgements

Foreword

Family History Cultures and Faiths is intended to give a background to the religious records which we use to trace our family history. It concentrates mostly on those from which the family tree can be constructed, showing where they can be obtained and how to interpret them. A selection of useful addresses and websites is given at the end of the book.

Many of the records described in the book are in the National Archives – but others are not. Chapter 9 goes in detail through those records which will be found at Kew, or have now been published or are going online. Records in the very important series RG 4–8 are going online from autumn 2007. See the birth, marriage and death records information page on the National Archives' website. Many other records are in county record offices or other archives, or are still with the religious groups that produced them.

The book also refers to various categories of records which family historians might expect but which were not produced by some denominations (such as records of infant baptism or confirmation).

This book is not about religion, though there is plenty of religious background in it. The author has had genealogy in his mind throughout and nothing here is intended to speak either for or against any particular belief. The book also deals with the generality of our ancestors, and for many of the generalizations given here it would be possible to find individuals who were exceptions. Indeed, one of the major points, repeated from time to time, is how difficult it is to know whether our specific ancestors fit the general template or not.

This book is also not intended for the complete beginner in family history. It is assumed that readers will understand the basic English record systems, including parish registers and civil registration, between 1500 and 1940. This book is not intended to explain what the records were, but rather why they took the form they did, how they differed from one group to another and how they apply to family historians. A beginner will benefit from reading it in conjunction with *Easy Family History* in the same series.

In chapter 8, **Abi Husainy** explains what

sources there are in the National Archives for tracing the background of those religious groups which only became large in England and Wales in the 20th century. Many of these records are concerned with these groups as immigrants or relate to their lives in the countries where they formerly lived. This is an area where our knowledge is increasing very fast, and this chapter contributes to the development of family history in this field.

All our ancestors were involved, to a greater or lesser degree, with religious practice. We cannot understand them without thinking about what they did and why they did it – which often turns out to be different from what we expected. Interestingly, it often helps us to think about what we do ourselves, and the reasons why we do it. These are our ancestors and – like it or not – they have made us what we are.

Michael Gandy

Note. A number of the chapters in this book are designed to be read on their own. It has therefore been necessary to repeat some points for the sake of those who may not read the book from beginning to end.

We (1) Govindbhai Jivanbhai Patel, aged 40 of Anand Bhuvan, Princess Street, Bombay 2 and (2) Manubhai Lallubhai Patel, aged 35 of 134, Dixit Road, Vile Parle, both of Bombay (India) do hereby state on solemn affirmation as hereunder:-

1. We say that Manilal Amthabhai Patel, now aged about 28, Indian by birth, residing in United Kingdom, is fully and intimately known to us since his childhood. As his father Amthabhai of Nimat, District Surat, Bombay State (India) happened to be intimately long known to us.

2. His father Amthabhai had married him to one Savitaben, daughter of Naranbhai Ranchhodbhai Patel on or about 24.2.57 of Sejwad, District Surat, Bombay State (India), the marriage ceremony was performed according to Hindu customs and Indian style whereat both of us had been present as invited by his father.

3. After their marriage both of them as husband and wife happened to imigrate to United Kingdom and settle there.

4. While in England some time after the imigration there arose acute disputes and differences and both of said Manilal and Savitaben could not live peacefully as husband and wife as they ought to be. The disputes and the greifs multiplied day by day without any end and solution thereof in the interest of the individual life of each Manilal and Savitaben mutually decided and agreed among themselves of their own accord and freewill to obtain divorce and ultimate seperation by consent.

5. Therefore by about the month of April 1958, the said Manilal and Savitaben obtained divorce by consent and freewill whereof Savitaben had been paid rupees three thousand five hundred and one (Rs.3501/-) as the price for the divorce togeher with the claim over the ornaments given up permantly by said Manilal whereunder all the ornaments that had been held by Savitaben upto the day of divorce became her property by virtue of the terms of divorce. Thus said Manilal and said Savitaben legally and customarily ceased to be the wife and husband effectively on and from tenth April 1958.

6. We further say that said Manilal and Savitaben belong to the Hindu Patidar community spread over the Bardoli Taluka of Surat district of Bombay state of the Union Government of India.

Introduction

Religion plays a great part in many people's lives; even those not themselves religious are often strongly affected by those who are, and this has always been the case. This book is concerned with the records which religious belief and practice have produced, and which can help us trace our family history.

The focus here is on the details of the records, not of the religion, and it is not intended to describe – let alone justify – any particular set of beliefs. Nor are we concerned with belief and practice in our own day. We are primarily concerned with the period 1500–1940, though neither of those dates has any special significance for religious history. The Reformation changed religious practice dramatically during the middle of the 16th century, but we shall want to refer back to the pre-Reformation Catholic Church from time to time. Chapter 8 considers the records of religious groups that established themselves more recently in

Britain and thus spans a later timeframe, approximately between 1880 and the 1960s.

There are many other practices which are not usually formally described as religious, or not treated as being separate religions, but which may still produce records. For example, many of our ancestors believed in witchcraft, whether for good or bad purposes, but they treated it as a deviant form of Christianity, not as a separate religion. However, it has generated many records, such as those of the Quarter Sessions and the Assizes, which may be useful in tracing family history.

Many common religious practices generate no records. For example, many Christians go to church on Sundays, or at other times, but there are no systematic records of attendance equivalent to a daily school register. However, *not* participating may generate records. In the 16th and early 17th centuries officials certainly kept an eye on who was present, and we therefore may have records of those who did not attend – with or without their reasons.

Religious practice, especially church attendance, was seen as a community activity, both morally and, for many years, legally binding. Many people also attended because their parents took them, or sent them, or because church was an important social meeting place or because attending would bring them social or economic advantages. None of this is inconsistent with also believing in the things they were doing.

There are a number of important pitfalls which we must try to avoid.

Thinking we know what they believed

Many people have a good general idea what various religious groups believe, but belief and practice change over time and it is usually wrong to read 21st-century attitudes back far into the past. On the other hand, it is also wrong to imagine that beliefs or practices that were current a little while ago had been unchanged for centuries. Most generations develop a style which answers the needs of their time. When thinking about our ancestors we need to know whom we are focusing on, and not make generalizations spanning centuries and entire countries – or even the world. Methodists in 1800 were not the same as Methodists in 1900; Catholics in 1950 were not the same as Catholics in 1850.

There is always a tendency to talk as though the old people were strict, possibly hidebound, and the young people were more tolerant and progressive. The very word 'progressive' is often used to mean that the future will be better than the past. However, there have been generations that were stricter than their parents. This was true of the generation that fought the Civil War. It was even more true in the 1830s and 1840s when respectable evangelical young people very much disapproved of the lax religion of their parents. In turn, many of their children disapproved of *them* as a generation arose in the 1860s which asserted the absolute truth and factual correctness of the Bible – including passages which their parents had been happy to accept as images.

Thinking they must have believed it all

The records we have often tell us what people did, but hardly ever tell us what they thought about it. People often talk about 'committed Anglicans', 'devout Catholics' or 'pious Methodists', but usually we have no way of knowing how strongly they felt. For that reason we must not make assumptions about what their attitude would have been to religious questions, particularly contentious family issues such as illegitimacy, divorce or marrying someone of another religion. Religious history books, including this one, tell us what the group generally is supposed to have believed, but we are concerned with one particular family who may or may not have been typical. Usually we cannot tell whether they were moderate, extreme or indifferent on any particular issue – except if we have documentary evidence of what they did.

Thinking they must have been consistent and unchanging

Religion is important to many people – but other things are also important, particularly money, love and class. Many people change their religious practice to keep in with people who may give them a job or leave them an inheritance. Individuals change their religion to bring them closer to someone they love, and many others change their style of worship to suit their social aspirations.

Other people simply develop as they get older and no longer believe, or believe less strongly, the things they were convinced of when they were young. Lots of family myths and legends include monster parents who break off relations with their children if they marry or convert out. In reality there are equal numbers of young people who nail their moral flag to the mast over some issue and demand

strict practice from parents who are reasonably easy-going. These stories are not handed
down so often, as the young people tend to
grow up and soften down – and forget.

Thinking you can say what the whole family's religion was

Parents with young children can usually define
the religion of their nuclear family, but as the
children grow up they may change their religion, perhaps to something drastically different. Family historians are often very respectful
of their ancestors' beliefs and these unexpected converts remain unknown (unless the
memory of them is handed down) because
researchers would not dream of looking at the
records of a religion they 'know' their family
would have had nothing to do with.

As adults, people then as now had to deal
with brothers and sisters and in-laws who had
changed religion, or had married in and not
changed religion. Children played with cousins
who had to do things which they did not have
to do – and just took it in their stride.
Differences in politics worked the same way –
and religion was often fairly closely bound in
with politics.

Judging whether they were right

This one really gets in the way. We like our ancestors to be decent people, and if they cannot be decent we want them to be disreputable in interesting ways. It can be hard if ancestors did things we really find distasteful.

There are a lot of religious and moral beliefs, both now and in the past, which we just do not share. Sometimes they seem ridiculous or illogical. Some are thoroughly unpleasant. Some ancestors seem to have been much stricter than we would approve of; others were easy-going or accepting of things that we would not tolerate.

Approving or disapproving of your ancestors is beside the point. They are the people they were and our job is to find out what their actions were and (much more difficult) what their logic was. We are trying to understand why they thought what they did. The reasons are often very interesting and sometimes they cause us to think about our own beliefs, but if you start to despise or dislike your ancestors then this is the wrong activity for you. Liking them and becoming all sentimental is not helpful either.

Accepting their beliefs too literally is often as bad as dismissing them out of hand. Many ancestors, from what we know them to have done, obviously did not take the strict line. Many religions have a spectrum of groups for those who are full-on, moderate or liberal. This is particularly true of groups who took their religion with them when they moved. Religious style and beliefs develop to meet the practical situation, and practices that worked well in one place have to be adapted to new circumstances. This is particularly true of religions which have moved from a country where they were mainstream to one where they were in a minority – perhaps a tiny minority – but it is equally true for people moving from the country to the town, from the north to the south, or indeed from one class to another. Individuals often adapt easily while the formal structures take much longer.

In fact, prejudice can be worst among people of the same religion as their ancestors. They often feel they have something to defend and may say 'But I am one of those and nobody of my religion would ever do that.' That sort of attitude seriously damages your research. If the evidence seems to indicate something, you have to accept it.

On the other hand, some modern researchers have minds which are almost too open. They are thus prepared to accept wild theories which are logically possible, but in practice utterly unlikely. Good background reading in social history is the answer, enabling you to set your ancestors in a realistic context.

Being hypnotized by the 'knowledge' we started with

Many people start family history research with some general knowledge, often picked up from school (when they were very young) or from films or from casual conversations – or from old relatives who did not really know but were used to laying down the law. Many people also use source books designed for beginners and risk picking up generalizations which do not in practice apply to their family. As in many areas of activity, the things one learns as a beginner are unduly simplified. Intermediate courses reveal that it is actually more complicated than that.

Many religious groups have an inherited history of how they were persecuted, and we often have to stand back and decide for ourselves how true this was. Sometimes there was indeed persecution, but on other occasions tolerant or indifferent people are cast as villains by people determined to have their own way all the time, including imposing their way on others. Martyrs are the life blood of any cause, and people who want to be hard done by can usually run rings round those who are easy-going. For many of our ancestors in the 17th century, religious 'freedom' meant the freedom to impose their beliefs on others. Hardly anyone believed in toleration.

At other times the inherited history of persecution is based on a few examples which may be true but were not widespread. Particular episodes are historical facts, but they have been adapted into everyone's inherited history. This applies particularly to the French *dragonnades*, the Irish Potato Famine and the Russian pogroms. All true – but not true for everybody, everywhere, at any date.

Films, novels and television are particularly unreliable. They are there to entertain and have no real obligation to get the history right. Dramatized versions of the past are even more unsafe because they make it look as if the past must have been like that. Many are consciously propaganda, and we need to be aware of that.

Forgetting that most people were Anglican

England has had many religious groups over the centuries but historically, interesting as they are, they were not very numerous as a percentage of the population – even when considered all together. Between the Reformation and 1800 (and with the exception of the Civil War and Commonwealth period) not more than five per cent of the population was outside the Anglican Church – and almost all of them appear in Anglican records anyway. For family historians looking back to the period between the 16th and the mid-20th century, Anglicanism is the default setting for records, whatever individuals may have believed.

I _Armand Lachapelle_ Minister of the _french Protestant Congregation in the Parish of Wandsworth in the County of Surrey_ do hereby certifie, That _Magdeleine Trevache_ of the Parish of _Wandsworth in ye County of Surrey aforesaid_ being Born out of the Queen's Allegiance, did on _Sunday_ the _six and twentieth_ Day of _june_ in the Year of Our Lord 1709 Receive the Sacrament of the _Lord's Supper_, which was by me administred to _Her the said Magdeleine Trevache_ in a Protestant or Reformed Congregation, being then Assembled in the said Church, Pursuant to an Act of Parliament, Entituled, _An Act for Naturalizing Foreign Protestants._ In Witness whereof I have hereunto subscribed my Hand the _Eighth_ Day of _july_ Anno Dom. 1709 _Armand Lachapelle minister of the french protestant congregation in wandsworth._

We James Capin de Barhays & Thomas de Livet Do severally make Oath that they did see the said _Magdeleine Trevache_ in the above-mentioned Certificate named; and who now present hath delivered the same into this Court, on the Day in the said Certificate mentioned, Receive the Sacrament of the _Lord's-Supper_ in a Protestant or Reformed Congregation Assembled in the said Church: And that they did see the said Certificate signed by the Minister, who administred the same to the said _Magdeleine Trevache._

J. T. de Barhays
thomas de Livet

Chapter 1

The historical background

Through the centuries, different denominations – even different religions – have waxed and waned in popularity. Historical events influenced religious fashions, and it is important in researching family history to understand the background to our ancestors' choices – the reasons that shaped their decisions and the implications of the beliefs they held for their everyday lives.

The majority of English people since the 16th century went to the Church of England (the Anglican Church) and we find their baptisms, marriages and burials in the parish registers. The Church of England rejected a lot of the old Roman Catholic beliefs and practices, but many people thought it had not gone far enough. They disliked the settlement of 1559 and the policy of Elizabeth I, who tried to found a national church that would include everyone by being flexible. These objectors were known as Puritans (because they thought the church needed to be purified further). This is not a book about religion as such, but some of the beliefs that separated the Puritans and Nonconformists from the Church of England are important for family historians.

By the early 17th century, Puritans had become a very articulate, influential and conspicuous group. However, they had decided to try and change the Church of England by staying within it so they almost all attended its services (many of them indeed were ministers) and went through the standard forms of baptism, marriage and burial, of which they did not really approve.

Thus for family historians there are no separate Nonconformist church records in the 16th and early 17th centuries. Sometimes we find Puritans presented before the ecclesiastical courts for expressing their opinions, but Puritans only really came under pressure in Charles I's reign (1625–49) after William Laud became Archbishop of Canterbury in 1633.

The Civil War and the Commonwealth

During the Civil War and the Commonwealth period (1642–60) the Anglican Church lost its power (temporarily) and the Puritans who disliked it were free to do what they wanted –

either inside or outside their parish churches. There were three main groups:

Presbyterians

Presbyterians believed in the authority of ministers, but not in the concept of bishops. They modelled themselves on the forms of the Scottish church founded by John Knox. These included very strict rules about behaviour, but in England they were never powerful enough to impose these on everybody.

Congregationalists

These are also known as Independents and Separatists (the three words refer to the same group). They believed in the 'priesthood of all believers', whereby all godly men (and to some extent women) were equal. They came together to hear the Bible read and explained and they invited respected ministers to lead them, but fundamentally they employed the minister. If they did not like his approach, they could dismiss him.

Baptists

Their distinguishing feature was refusing to baptize children. Instead, they practised adult 'believers' baptism'. For family historians this makes them the most difficult group to trace.

Other groups arose during the same period: *Ranters*, *Levellers*, *Seekers*, *Fifth Monarchy Men*. They were very religious and there is a lot of material on individuals, but they did not keep records about their families. None of these groups lasted beyond 1660 and most had no interest in formal church structures.

However, another group, the *Muggletonians*, did survive. They were always very few in number but only finally died out in 1979. Their records are now in the British Library.

The only group to survive this period in large numbers were the *Quakers*, whose numbers exploded dramatically in the 1650s.

Quakers
Quakers did not believe in any church struc-tures – or any ministers – at all, but their belief in equality without leaders led them to develop a structure of committees with secretaries recording decisions (arrived at by consensus – Quakers would never vote) and a central head-quarters in London. Lots of their records have been handed down and we can often say with confidence what Quakers thought or did. In fact, the other groups often thought and did very much the same – and may have kept

records of it at the time – but each meeting was independent and for the most part their records have not survived.

After 1660

After the restoration of the monarchy in 1660, an Anglican parliament required ministers to use the Book of Common Prayer without alteration and to accept the principle of ordination. Many people left the Church of England and for the next 30 years there was a lot of pressure on them to conform. A great many were presented at Quarter Sessions for their refusal to attend church, and those lists of names are our only systematic source for identifying the ordinary people. These lists have to be used with care. Firstly, some magistrates or ministers were keener than others to punish those who were breaking the law. Secondly, the authorities often did not enquire what specific reasons they had for not obeying the law, with the result that all the various groups are mixed together and the same list may contain Baptists, Quakers and Catholics.

All the main denominations have been thoroughly researched, often by local historians or people interested in general theological or political trends. These researchers were often not interested in the names as such and did not have our specific knowledge about individual families. Even if you are confident you know to which type of Nonconformity your ancestors belonged, it is always worth searching publications about all groups. Your Baptist ancestors may be in a list published by a Catholic or Quaker society – and vice versa.

Moreover, family historians naturally think in terms of families and long-term habits, but both individuals and groups may chop and change. My family in Great Budworth, Cheshire, were Puritan Anglicans until the Civil War, then Baptists. In 1654 my ancestors William and Edward Gandy converted to Quakerism while their uncle Hugh Gandy and his children stayed Baptist. Other relatives stayed Anglican. For the next hundred years the Quaker Gandys are easy to trace, but the family tree of the Baptist branch has lots of gaps and uncertainties since there are no records at all of whatever meetings they attended.

After 1689

Noncomformists achieved a legal assurance of toleration through the Act of Settlement in 1689, and in 1691 they were granted permission to meet (and build separate buildings if they wanted) provided they registered their meeting places at Quarter Sessions. From this time on we begin to get registers of baptism (though very few go back this far). However, a comparison of the known baptism registers (almost all in the National Archives in series RG 4 and indexed on the Mormon website FamilySearch.org) with the known registrations of meetings (again at the National Archives, this time in series RG 31) is depressing. In most counties there were dozens, even hundreds, of meetings registered for which no surviving records are known. Especially if they just met in someone's house, we often have no evidence how long the meeting continued, how many people went to it, or whether they ever kept any records.

Methodists
Between 1700 and about 1760 Nonconformist numbers went down, but they rose again later in that century and increased dramatically when John Wesley's Methodists came out of the Church of England and became a separate organization in the 1780s. They, too, were well organized and fairly centralized, and quickly began to keep records. However, Methodists are not strictly Nonconformists. They had fallen

out with the Anglicans for reasons which had nothing to do with either theology or liturgy, and in their early days were often willing to go to Anglican services as well as their own.

The 19th century

In the 19th century Nonconformist numbers grew dramatically, but general church attendance began to decline. The newcomers had no allegiance to the ancient history of their denomination and there was often little difference between ordinary Nonconformist chapels – with their emphasis on hymn singing and the sermon – and the local Anglican church if it was evangelical and 'low'. People were often willing to change denomination fairly easily if other factors (such as a more convenient location) made it sensible. Both groups equally distrusted the 'high' Anglo-Catholics with their emphasis on the sacraments and ceremonial.

Non-Christian religions

Until the 20th century the number of non-Christians, except for Jews, was a tiny proportion of the population. Almost all were temporary residents or new arrivals, and the vast majority were men. If they married and founded families, their children and descendants almost certainly became Christian within a generation. We are not concerned here with the records of newcomers as 'foreigners', but with the question of what non-Christian religious records there may be which would be useful for tracing a family tree.

Those practising other religions in past centuries came almost entirely from abroad. At various times there were quite a number, but they were concentrated in London or in the major ports, including Bristol and later Liverpool. Many were transitory, and in the 17th and 18th centuries numbers were very low. By the mid- and late 19th century there were many thousands overall, but they can be difficult to identify. Fortunately we do not have to identify an entire group, merely to recognize whether specific relatives of ours fall into any of the likely categories.

Here a word of warning. Often family myths have developed based on an odd surname or generalizations about a common one and the family have guessed themselves into being French or German or Jewish (the three most usual suspects).

Recent developments in DNA have also opened people's minds to the possibility that our distant ancestors came from Egypt or

Armenia or equally far away. Yes, absolutely –
but not within a recent, traceable time frame.
The vast majority of British people's ancestors
were in Britain at least as far back as 1600 and
were Christian, mostly Anglican. If you have
evidence that your ancestor was one of many
other possibilities, obviously you must go with
that, but otherwise it is sensible to assume the
vastly more probable option.

The largest group who might have a non-
Christian religion were foreign merchants.
These might live in Britain for some years without feeling that they were permanent settlers.
They may have brought wives with them, or
acquired wives from home. Those few who
married British women would be more likely to
settle permanently. Many of these (though
that is not to imply that numbers were large)
were from the old Turkish Empire and probably
Muslim; they were the counterparts of the
British merchants who lived for long periods in
places such as Constantinople and Aleppo.
There were also Greeks and Armenians,
though they were Christians. There were
Parsees, or Parsis, who were Zoroastrian and
founded a society in Britain in 1861 with a
burial ground at Woking. There were also
Bahai from Persia. An important leader died in

London and was buried at New Southgate Cemetery on the northern outskirts. Since then many Bahai have chosen to be buried there in the same section.

Ambassadorial staff are a smaller group still. Like the others mentioned above, they had status (and money) and are likely to have been visible and attractively exotic. If they practised their religion in their own homes, no one will have questioned their right to do so.

Further down the social scale the largest group was sailors, many from India and largely in the East End of London where they were mostly connected with the East India Company ships. These were known as Lascars, originally derived from the word *askari* meaning, strangely enough, a soldier.

Liverpool and Bristol had few Lascars but more Caribbeans, probably coming in on the West Indian merchant ships. They are likely to have been Christians who brought over a good deal of religious baggage from their African heritage. Whatever they may have practised privately, they were not organized into religious congregations, and the most likely religious record of them in this country will be their burial in an Anglican or borough cemetery.

Many West Indian planters and traders

brought their servants with them – servants or slaves – but there was also quite a large class of negro servants permanently attached to English families. In the mid-18th century a little black boy was quite a fashionable accessory for a lady. Some Indians came as body servants to retiring East India Company men.

We are not here concerned with ethnicity, nor with the history of religion in other countries, but in the 17th and early 18th centuries it was not generally the custom to baptize the babies of slaves, either in North America or in the Caribbean. We therefore find quite a large number of baptisms of adults in the London registers, and a few elsewhere. It seems likely, however, that these were not recent converts to Christianity from some other religion. Rather they were people who were in a Christian setting abroad, but had not been baptized there. However, the entries do not usually say and we must not assume.

Towards the middle and end of the 19th century a number of Chinese also settled in London and other ports, but I am not aware of any formal records relating to their temples and shrines.

Both the Lascars (and other sailors) and the Chinese were very largely single men. They may have married, but their wives were most likely to have been English or Irish and their children will mostly have been absorbed into the large class who were technically Anglican but not very church-attending. Now that the open censuses are online, it is easy to search by birthplace and establish how many people had come from countries where religions other than Christianity were mainstream. However, birthplace is not actually any indication of ethnicity and many religions were linked very closely to specific ethnic groups. None of the censuses now open asked any question about religious affiliation.

There was also a class of more educated men who came to Britain to study. This applies particularly to Indians who probably expected to go home after their education (or training) was finished. Many did, but not all.

The records of civil service applications from approximately 1855 to 1914 give evidence of birth and contain at least one astrological chart. These are at the Society of Genealogists. See 'Irreplaceable Evidence of Age for the Civil Service Commission', Elisabeth McDougall and Dick Mynott (*Genealogists' Magazine*, vol. 27, no. 7, September 2002).

There were far fewer isolated women,

though there were a number of Caribbean female servants who were probably Christian. There were, however, a small number of Indian wives who came to England when their husbands came home. Before the 1820s it was very common for Europeans to partner up with a local woman. The East India Company strongly encouraged this and the women were indeed wives, properly married. The intention, however, was to encourage children who would combine loyalty to Britain through their fathers with acclimatization to the Indian climate, diseases, food etc. through their mothers – so it was expected that the men would stay in India, not that their wives would migrate to Britain. Many of the women became Christians, though no doubt they retained many of their old beliefs.

The officer class and the senior clerks and merchants also acquired Indian women, often in long-term relationships. They are not likely to have married them, but the relationships were widespread and wholly acceptable in India, as were the children. These are men who may well have come home if they lived long enough to retire and some brought their wives (possibly mere 'wives') with them. These women had in many cases been baptized, and if they retained any practices from their former religions, these would be practised domestically and inconspicuously. No congregations, no public records.

Since the Second World War the number of other religions in Britain has risen very substantially. In chapter 8 Abi Husainy of the National Archives gives some indication of the type of records that are available at Kew regarding these burgeoning cultures, communities and faiths. However, other than for Jews, we are not aware of any non-Christian genealogical religious records for the period 1500–1940 which have been deposited publicly or published. No non-Christian congregations figure in the 1851 religious census, for example, and no non-Christian meeting places were registered for marriages before 1898. There were no private non-Christian burial grounds. With the steady secularization of record-keeping in the 19th century, there was no problem with the marriages of non-Christians in register offices or burials of non-Christians in the unconsecrated sections of public cemeteries. They could be interred according to their own rites and could raise monuments in their own style. There was something of a problem for those groups which did not dispose of their dead by burial (page 225), but cremation was made legal in 1904.

A number of British people were converted (most not through any formal ceremony) to some form of the wisdom of the East, and from the 1880s the work of people such as the Theosophists spread among a certain stratum of the middle class. Some had been in India, but many were convinced by reading. This ran parallel to the development of Spiritualism which was sometimes based on eastern philosophy and sometimes an outcrop of Christianity. In practice, these transformed the lives of individuals, but did not lead to congregations of families. Many people were willing to cherry-pick, largely from forms of Buddhism, but no substantial body of Asian Buddhists settled in this country up to the Second World War. Yoga and Spiritualism became very popular in the 1920s.

Gypsies

The only large group of families in England with non-Christian customs were the gypsies. The first gypsies in the British Isles were in Scotland in the 15th century, but they are not recorded in England until early in the following century. They came originally from northern India and preserved a number of attitudes and customs. However, they did not form religious congregations nor maintain any independent religious records; for tracing them we are dependent on the standard records of Anglican genealogy.

In practice, the original 'Romany' families were mixed with large numbers of people who travelled around for other reasons, and often did so for generations. Most gypsies did not wander randomly; they had fairly fixed routes and timetables and were not strangers in their regular haunts. Many of them had their children baptized, if only to establish settlement. It is hard to say what percentage of Romanies married according to their own customs or disposed of their dead in their own way, but certainly a great many of their marriages and burials are in the Anglican registers. Moreover, there was always intermarriage with settled people.

Finding the baptisms and marriages of gypsies was more of a problem before there were large-scale indexes such as the Mormon FamilySearch and the National Burial Index. As to burial, it is common to say that gypsy ancestry is complicated by the numbers of burial entries for nameless strangers. However, my feeling is that these refer to the many other people who were travelling alone, for example

What's in a name?

Some gypsies used their mother's name rather than their father's despite being married (whether in the Anglican Church or by their own customs). Thus Sarah Carus was married in 1840 and gave her father as John Moore – which at first sight implies illegitimacy. However, her parents, John Moore and Elizabeth Carus, had married in 1818 – four years before she was born.

men looking for work, soldiers and sailors walking home to their relatives, widows or abandoned women and their children, or discharged servant girls trying to get to a place where they had friends. Any of these might die in a barn or an inn and leave no one to say who they were. Gypsies are not in that sort of category. Nor were circus and fairground folk with whom gypsies had a substantial overlap, or river and canal folk with whom there was much less. All these people travelled in groups. If they died and their relatives chose to bring them to the church for burial, they would be perfectly able to state their names. See *My Ancestors were Gypsies*, Sharon Floate (Society of Genealogists, 1999).

Witches, wiccans and druids

Some people nowadays would want to claim witches or wiccans or druids as having a separate religion. However, our ancestors between 1500 and 1940 saw witches as an evil form of Christian, in contrast to herbalists and healers who practised legitimate folk cures. Some medical treatments, such as charms for warts, hovered perilously between the two. The revival of druidism in Wales in the late 19th century was social or cultural or nationalistic, and had nothing to do with religion.

The patterns of religious practice in Britain have varied from century to century, although beliefs are much harder to quantify. For family historians, the historical context determines not only what was prevailing when, but also what records have remained for us to explore. As well as the broader picture, researchers need an understanding of the religious practices themselves to discover what records were ever available and what we might now expect to find. In the next chapter I shall look at the religious acts that many of our ancestors performed, with the emphasis on whether there might be any records to assist family historians, and if so of what sort.

D E N° 241

THESE are to certify, That _John Randell_
and _Margret Randell_ ~~son~~ of _Benjamin Randell_ his Wife, who was Daughter of
Rev. Mr. Graham & Mary Graham was Born in _Sunderland_
in the Parish of _St. ———_
in the County of _Durham_ in the Year One Thousand Eight
Day of _January_ ——— the _fourteenth_
Hundred and Six at whose Birth we were present

~~ Mary Forsyth
Ann Nineghton 242

Registered at Dr. WILLIAMS's Library, Redcross-Street, near Cripplegate, London.
July 8th 1812   Thos Morgan   Register

Chapter 2

Life stages and religious records

Since 1534 the official religion of England has been the Church of England (described using the adjective Anglican). The monarch is head of the Church and everyone born here is assumed to be a member of that church unless they or their parents declare themselves to be of some other religion – or none. Until 1689 it was illegal not to be part of the Church of England, but since then there has been much wider (though not complete) freedom of worship. Catholicism remained illegal until 1778 (and there are still some anti-Catholic laws). Unitarianism (not believing in the Trinity) remained illegal until 1813.

The Church of England had taken over from Catholicism (usually called Roman Catholicism until the second half of the 20th century). The word 'catholic' means universal and the Anglican Church also claimed to be catholic in that sense. The establishment of the Anglican

Church was part of the Protestant Reformation of the 16th century, but its members had a great spectrum of beliefs, from those who believed almost everything that Catholics believed but rejected the headship of the Pope to those who thought that the Church of England was full of errors and needed a great deal of purifying. At first these people remained inside the Anglican Church, becoming known as Puritans, but later they crystallized as a number of denominations outside the Anglican Church. The largest were the Presbyterians, Congregationalists (also known as Separatists or Independents), Baptists and Quakers, but there were other much smaller groups such as Muggletonians and Unitarians.

Methodists did not form a separate denomination until 1787 and they took almost all their initial beliefs and practices from the Anglican Church. Thus most of the references we shall make to Nonconformists do not refer to them.

From the 1660s until the late 18th century, if not later, Protestants outside the Church of England often called themselves dissenters, emphasizing their disagreement with the official church. They were also called Nonconformists, also emphasizing their refusal to be part of the mainstream. From the early 19th century the term 'dissenter' fell into disuse for any contemporary group, but the words are pretty well interchangeable.

England and Wales were united administratively in 1534 and the situation was basically the same until 1870 when the Church of Wales was disestablished – that is, ceased to be the official religion of that part of the United Kingdom. However, the Church of England in Wales (later called the Church of Wales) was very weak and a higher percentage of the population attended a Nonconformist meeting. This is in large part due to the lack of a substantial landed aristocracy, gentry or even upper middle class in Wales. The land and the economy were too poor to provide good incomes or good careers, with the result that many young people left for England.

The situation was quite different in Scotland and Ireland, but this book does not focus on those countries. We shall refer to them from time to time, but not systematically.

Despite their disagreements, all the Christian denominations of England and Wales took a view over the following ceremonies to mark various stages in life. Many of them did not mark them all, but they all knew that others did and therefore developed theological explanations for either doing them or not doing them.

Seven of the ceremonies described below – baptism, confirmation, holy communion (also called Eucharist), penance, anointing of the sick, holy order (often called holy orders) and matrimony – were called sacraments by the Catholics who considered them 'indelible marks on the soul'. Anglicans considered there were only two sacraments: baptism and holy communion. Most other denominations did not believe in the concept of sacraments, though many went through the same ceremonies (albeit with a different emphasis).

The following summaries apply above all to the 16th, 17th and early 18th centuries. They were all pretty watered down by the 19th century. Even the Baptists (who would not baptize babies) mostly developed a service of dedication which served the same social purpose.

Most of the denominations had a wide spectrum of belief. The Anglicans had a full-blown organization, but made a virtue of not insisting that everyone believed or behaved in the same way. Catholics had a centralized system, but for much of the period from 1559 to 1778 they were too weak to impose it. Almost all the other groups had a theology which believed that every congregation – even every individual –

was independent. Thus there were many hundreds of Baptist meetings, but it is not possible to say what the Baptist Church as an entity believed, because there was no such thing. The same applied to Presbyterians and Independents. In principle it applied to Quakers as well, but they became very bureaucratic and very articulate about their beliefs. In theory they would not impose these ideas on anyone else, but they were prepared to 'withdraw' from people who did not see things their way.

Baptisms, christenings and dedications

Most Christian denominations believed in the concept of original sin, the idea that, because of the sin of Adam, everyone is damned unless... At this point various groups had different opinions and this is not a book on theology. For most people, however, baptism came into it at some stage.

There were two positions as regards admission to the Church and salvation by water. Catholics, Anglicans and many Nonconformists believed in infant baptism. Clearly an infant could not have belief, but being saved 'by water' meant that children dying below the age of reason would be able to go to heaven innocent of sin. Catholics had a theology of limbo for unbaptized children, but all the Protestant churches rejected this.

In our period Catholics tended to baptize more quickly than Anglicans or others and baptism often took place at the child's home – possibly even in the mother's bedroom since women stayed in bed much longer after childbirth than they do in our day. Thus an entry of baptism in a Catholic register may not refer to a ceremony in a church or chapel.

Anglicans and most of the other Protestant denominations believed in infant baptism, but were content to wait a few weeks until the mother was well enough to come to church. However, if a baby was thought likely to die then it could be quickly baptized wherever it was, by a minister if possible but otherwise by the midwife or indeed anybody in an emergency. These baptisms are recorded as 'private baptisms' or 'half-baptisms'. If the baby died it could have burial as an infant Christian, and if it lived the child would get public baptism later.

Some Protestant denominations rejected the concept of infant baptism. These were the ones who believed that children could not be saved until they were old enough to accept for themselves or, more usually, to have the conviction that they were marked out for salvation by God's grace. They would then choose to be baptized as an act of public witness.

For family historians the records of infant baptism are very important. For the churches at the time it was thought important to have a record of something that the child would not remember. However, Catholic children had been baptized for centuries without anyone feeling the need to record the fact, and the establishment of parish registers was part of the church's (and state's) wish to police the community and check who was obeying the law. In England parish registers were ordered to be kept from 1538, but this was a tendency which was Europe-wide.

In the 16th and early 17th century it was a legal requirement to have children baptized, but this died away in practice after the mid-17th century. However, the vast majority of people continued to bring their children to baptism if only (though not only) because a record of baptism was the vital proof of where a child was born for purposes of settlement and poor relief. Over the centuries there were attempts to make the parish register a record of all children, including those not baptized or baptized by other ministers. In 1696 the law required the minister to record all children and in some

Lancashire parishes in the 1700s we find records of Catholic baptisms. In general this move was not successful and Anglican registers remained records of Anglican baptisms. However, because of the settlement question you may reasonably assume, certainly for ordinary families, that a child was born in the parish where it was baptized unless the register says otherwise.

Non-Anglican congregations must often have kept registers of the baptisms their ministers performed, or ministers may have kept personal registers. Those which existed at the end of the 1830s were almost all handed into public keeping and are now in the National Archives at Kew in series RG 4–8. They are widely available on microfilm; many have been transcribed and published. A simplified index to most of them is available on the Mormon website FamilySearch.org.

Many earlier registers may have existed and have been lost. However, the people who compiled those registers knew that their records were purely informal and never expected that they would serve any purpose. Nonconformists were mostly literate people and it was natural to expect that parents would keep a record of their own children's births and baptisms. These often survive inside Bibles or Prayer Books or elsewhere, but there is no systematic place to look. Mrs Rena King, 16 Upper Shott, Cheshunt, Herts EN7 6DR has collected many entries from family Bibles.

The words baptism and christening are both used to describe the same ceremony. The technical difference between these two words is that baptism refers to the ceremony of reception into the church and christening refers to the name that was usually given at infant baptism. In practice they can be used interchangeably when talking of young babies, but you should not use the word christening when talking of adults.

These days people tend to announce the name of the child as soon as it is decided, including before the birth. In the past many people stuck to the formal rule that the baby did not have a name until it had received it at baptism. Thus the burials of unbaptized babies usually do not give a name, and census returns often give no name for a baby of a few days or even a few weeks.

It was generally the custom for the father to state what the baby's name was to be (that does not necessarily mean that he had chosen it). His acceptance of that role was felt to be a public declaration that he agreed he was the father. If he had any doubts or was certain that he was not and intended to say so, then that was the moment to go public. Our ancestors were concerned with legal parenthood rather than genetic parenthood, and the point was that he was accepting the legal obligation to support the child financially and the child's right to be his legitimate heir.

The word legitimate means 'according to the law' and many statements of parenthood (not so often in baptism registers, but in wills and court cases) include a phrase like 'his natural and legitimate son' – making the point that he had fathered the baby biologically and that he and the mother were married.

England had no binding social customs about naming patterns. One can often see that in practice children have been named for relatives, but this is hindsight. Many people may indeed have named their eldest children after themselves or their parents, but this was a personal decision, possibly influenced by others! It was very common to name children after a godparent of the same sex.

See *Using Baptism Records for Family Historians*, Pauline Litton (Federation of Family History Societies, 1996).

Godparents

It was pretty well universal for a child to have godparents who undertook the responsibility of keeping an eye on the child's spiritual and moral development. There were no formal duties attached to this and it was purely personal to the people concerned whether they actually did anything. There was likely to be at least one man and one woman.

Unfortunately, Anglican registers hardly ever tell us who the godparents were. There certainly were some, but we have to gather their names incidentally from other sources. The most important of these is wills, since many people left money to their godchildren and stated the relationship. This means that it is easier to trace what godchildren an adult had than what godparents a child had.

Catholics and non-Anglicans took the concept of godparents more seriously and their registers often name the godparents – in Catholic registers they are often called sponsors. From these we can see that godparents were often close relatives and that couples often stood as godparents to each other's children over a period of time. It was more practical to have young godparents than old ones since they were clearly a backstop in case the parents died. Godparents might indeed be pretty young, and many teenagers were god-parents to their nephews and nieces.

The relationship of godparent was more binding in continental Catholic countries and a relationship of mutual friendship and moral commitment was deepened between the adults concerned. The words *compadre* and *commadre* in Spanish describe this relation-ship, and there are equivalent words in many southern Mediterranean languages. In English the word 'gossip' (sibling in God) describes the relationship between two people of whom one had stood as godparent to another's child, and in many villages the relationship of godparents must have tied enormous numbers of people to-gether in ways which are usually invisible to us.

It is important to follow godparents up if possible.

Churching

Anglican women who had given birth came to church to give thanks for a safe delivery and to be purified. This was very, very common indeed and may be referred to anecdotally, but did not often generate any records. A few vic-ars noted it occasionally, for example the vicar of St Nicholas, Chiswick, Middlesex.

Adoption

Technically there was no such thing until 1926. However, vast numbers of men and women brought up children to whom they were not related, mostly their stepchildren. It was not expected that such children would take their stepfather's surname, and any suggestion that they did should be backed up with proof. As

---

Did you know?

People often talk about children being adopted, but there was no formal procedure for doing this until 1926. Taking other people's children to live with you was fairly common, but they were often relatives such as nephews and nieces whose parents had died or who had more children than they could cope with. There was no general expectation that the adults would allow people to think that the child had been born to them (as there often was between the 1940s and the 1970s). Nor was illegitimacy so much of a stigma as it was in the mid-20th century, and there must have been fewer cases where an illegitimate grandchild grew up thinking its mother was its sister. Illegitimacy was so common in the 19th century that it is hard to believe that can often have happened, but one certainly sees cases where an illegitimate bride or groom gives their grandfather as their father on the marriage certificate. We usually cannot know whether they believed it or were covering an awkward situation with a white lie.

you go back before 1900, the less and less likely it becomes.

Catechism

The catechism is not a ceremony, but a book setting out the beliefs of the Anglican Church. Catholics had a different catechism, but in both cases young people were taught it and expected to be examined in it at confirmation. The Nonconformists had no equivalent though the Westminster Confession of Faith (1648) summed up the position for many of them.

Attendance at Sunday school

Taking children out of church for the period of the sermon developed as children came to be seen as separate entities and not just small adults. The idea of separate services or meetings for children grew, and in the 19th century these were important for almost all denominations. A separate Sunday school, outside church time, was supposed to attract children of non-attenders and often shaded over from Bible knowledge to work on reading and writing. A very large number of young people whose parents rarely attended church or chapel services attended Sunday school.

A number of religious organizations, or organizations with a religious undertone, developed around 1900, from Pathfinders and the Church Lads Brigade to the Boy Scouts and Girl Guides. These were often attached to a church and attended services, perhaps once a month. However, some were about character development rather than religious beliefs. These overlapped with church activities of an even less religious nature, such as church football teams.

Sunday school registers and logs sometimes survive. Sunday school children's activities, prizes, outings and performances often figure in church newsletters and magazines and may even be referred to in the local newspapers. Many people first find out which church their ancestors attended because they have a Bible or Prayer Book given to them for scripture knowledge or good attendance.

Confirmation

Anglican and Catholic children who had been baptized as infants were expected to confirm their belief when they got old enough. In practice this was likely to occur when the bishop visited the parish. He might ask them questions or he might take the vicar's word that he had examined them. After confirmation the young people would take communion for the first time and from then on were considered independent adults (from the religious point of view) and not the subjects of their parents. However, many teenagers were away from home as servants or apprentices and young people were expected to follow the religious practices of the house where they lived. The word 'family' was used to mean people who lived in the same household, regardless of whether there was a blood connection.

The age of confirmation varied, but for Anglicans it tended to be in the early teens. For Catholic children it was often younger, but until the 19th century confirmation for Catholics was often not available in England; people were confirmed when they could be.

During the 19th century Catholics began to separate the ceremony of confirmation (which needed a more adult understanding of the cat-echism) from taking holy communion and the separate ceremony of First Communion devel-oped. This was not the case for Anglicans.

Catholics kept proper records of confirma-tion and these include the special religious name that each child took. These names usu-ally have no family significance at all, but were the names of saints. There may be a clue to the child's (or the family's) particular religious devotion in the name of the saint chosen.

It is very rare to find any records of Anglican confirmations before the end of the 19th century. We may assume that it happened, but be unable to prove it unless there is a casual record in a diary or letter. Bishops' diaries are likely to record when and where they confirmed, but not to name the young people.

Church membership, conversion and attendance

The Nonconformist churches did not have a ceremony of confirmation. For those who did not baptize children, there was nothing to confirm. The young people underwent believers' baptism when they wanted to, but for the most part it was not thought necessary to record this. However, there was certainly a point at which children brought up in the church became independent members.

Anglicans and Catholics believed that all baptized people were Christians and that meant in practice almost everybody. The Nonconformist congregations, however, thought of proper Christians as a small percentage of the population, surrounded by people who were not proper Christians even if they thought they were. Most congregations were independent of all others and consisted of members (whose religious credentials were acceptable) and attenders or hearers who might or might not be approved but who would hopefully eventually be converted, convinced, born again (or whatever phrase the congregation used) and would then seek to be accepted as members. Members spoke at church meetings, accepted offices, went on the committees and accepted a financial responsibility for the expenses of the minister's salary and running the meeting.

Young people who had been brought up in the church were sooner or later accepted as adult members on the basis of their track record of behaviour and some level of religious examination in the doctrines of the group. This may have been recorded or it may be that their names simply begin to appear on the lists of members that were certainly kept, if only for financial purposes.

Members of a congregation who moved would find another congregation and, sooner or later, apply to become members of that. They would expect to obtain some sort of religious character reference from their previous congregation. If the new congregation kept a note that this had been seen then it is obviously vital evidence of where the newcomers had come from. The meeting they were leaving may also have recorded that they had asked for a recommendation and been given it.

Members might be dismissed from membership for bad behaviour or for believing unsuitable things. This did not necessarily mean that they ceased to attend, only that they had been downgraded. The minister and elders often hoped that they would see the error of their ways and could be re-admitted to membership in due course.

Anglicans and Catholics were happy to receive converts. Quakers and Baptist converts (the latter were often called Anabaptists) were usually baptized and the entry will appear in the baptism register. The phraseology may differ if they were being received from another branch of the Christian church which practised baptism since both Anglicans and Catholics (the two main groups involved) more or less accepted each other's baptisms. Catholic entries are likely to say (in Latin) 'conditional baptism' and give a birth date showing the person was an adult. Anglican entries may say that the convert was received or abjured the errors of the Roman Church rather than that he or she was baptized – but the entry is still in the baptism register. An age may be given but not a birth date.

A small number of people were received from other religions and there are quite a large number of entries for slaves and servants from India, Africa, the American colonies or the West Indies. Usually we cannot tell if they were temporary or permanent residents. They were often baptized Scipio or Caesar in honour of two famous Roman figures who were thought to have been black.

Tithes

These are not religious acts as such, but they may produce records showing that our ancestors were connected with particular churches.

Churches and ministers had to be paid for. The Anglican Church was entitled to tithes, a payment based on the income of property owners (or property holders if that was in the terms of the lease). In the second half of the 17th century Quakers witnessed very strongly against tithes. Many were sued by their parish ministers and appear in court or even prison records. However, their lead was not followed.

By the early 19th century the resentment of tithes was much stronger among those who did not attend the Anglican Church and had no wish to pay towards it. Eventually most tithes were commuted for a money payment.

These are really records of land and not appropriate to this book. The same applies to other records of church land, whether at diocesan or parish level.

Pew rents and collections

Medieval churches did not have many seats. For the congregation services were not very participatory and people walked or knelt or prayed or talked often in a fairly unstructured way – the essential point was to be present as part of the community while the priests did their job. A bell rang when the congregation's attention was needed.

This changed at the Reformation as most churches now had readings and sermons which were intended to be listened to. Sermons could be very long indeed and the congregation could not be expected to stand still for an hour – or two! Thus stools and benches began to appear.

The lack of movement meant that people could get cold, and it was not long before boxed pews developed, to be rented to those who could afford them. These became private, in effect, and lockable.

Many parish records contain references to pew rents and plans of which pews were rented to which parishioners. Richard Gough's *History of Myddle* describes all the inhabitants of a parish in 1700 by going systematically round the pews describing their occupants.

In country parishes there was room for everybody in one way or another, but in town churches by the 18th and 19th centuries it was not expected that everybody would come to services. There were very few 'free' seats, and many of them were likely to be allocated to children from the orphanage or old people from the almshouse. Those who wanted to increase church attendance pointed to this as a serious discouragement and there was a campaign for more free seats.

Slowly the concept of private pews died away. Naturally this left churches with a funding problem which was solved by taking up a regular collection. There are no records of who gave to these. However, churches also took up other subscriptions, either for issues of their own, such as church maintenance, or for good causes, and there are often lists of those who subscribed or gave. They may be informal, but it was also common practice to publish them so that people could see who had given what.

Where children were involved, there might be a small prize for the child who had collected the most. These are late 19th- and even 20th-century practices. By this time many churches and chapels were producing church magazines, but these do not often survive.

Holy communion

In the Anglican Church communion was likely to take place about once a month. In the Catholic Church it was more frequent, but we seldom find records of those who went to communion and there were no formalities.

Many of the Nonconformist chapels only had communion rarely and only admitted members or people whose religious standing was impeccable. The minister or elders gave out communion tokens in advance to those who were acceptable and one of the disciplinary procedures against people behaving badly was to withhold their communion tokens. This was a very public criticism.

We do not often find lists of those who were admitted to communion in the churches which have membership, but where the disciplinary records survive they are likely to record the names of those who were excluded – and why. In principle all members will have gone to communion, but there was long-term debate between those churches who wanted to restrict communion to members and those who were prepared to offer communion to anyone who wanted it.

From 1672 (the first Test Act) there was a shopping list of activities for which people had to present evidence that they were members of the Church of England. Here the word 'members' is used in a very loose sense. The evidence required was a certificate to say that the person concerned had taken Anglican communion once in the preceding year. Communion certificates (usually called sacrament certificates) turn up quite often in Quarter Sessions or in parish records. It is simpler to say that if a person is known to have, for example, attended Oxford or Cambridge University then he must have been an Anglican, or been prepared to go through the motions, whether we find a certificate or not. Lower middle class and working class people had little need of sacrament certificates since they did not do the things for which they were necessary.

In the 18th and 19th centuries many committed dissenters were perfectly able to make the distinction between the parish as a religious entity (with which they would have little to do) and the parish as an administrative unit collecting the poor rates and giving out poor relief. Even the Quakers, who objected to tithes in support of a 'hireling ministry', had no objection to paying their rates to the parish Overseers of the Poor.

Behaviour

It is perhaps not quite right to include a section on behaviour in this list, but most of the Nonconformist churches had a clear view that proper Christians would behave themselves and therefore took bad behaviour (including wrong belief) as a sign that an individual was not a proper Christian. The standards varied from congregation to congregation and were not always along the lines we may imagine. For example, since Christians expected that God would be with them, failures in business were a suspicious sign that a man's Christian life might not be up to scratch, and congregations took a very dim view of bankruptcy.

The Church of England had ecclesiastical courts which would investigate anyone accused of religious or moral crimes – blasphemy, heresy, bigamy, adultery, general religious unruliness – and also looked at annulment, separation and divorce (see below). However, simple non-attendance at church was not dealt with by the ecclesiastical courts as it was against the law of the land. It appears in the records of Quarter Sessions or, in more extreme cases, the Assizes.

From 1559 to 1642 the Puritans who objected to the liturgy and theology of the Church of England attempted to influence it from the inside. The vast, vast majority did not refuse to come to church, and people cited for non-attendance before Quarter Sessions are likely to be Catholics if they had a religious reason. Others were those who just preferred to play bowls or sit in the alehouse.

One of the most important planks of Puritan belief was the vital importance of Sunday as 'the Lord's Day'. It should be given to church attendance and religious study and the Puritans lobbied hard for other activities to be stopped – not only entertainments such as football, but also useful activity enshrined in law, particular archery. In the towns, the distinction between work and not-work was usually fairly clear, and Puritan pressure offered protection to working people whose employers thought they might as well go back to work after the church services. Very few people thought that domestic servants should not work on Sundays the same as every other day.

Puritans emphasized Sundays, but the other side of the coin was that they thought religious activity on other days of the week was wrong: 'Six days shalt thou labour.' The Anglicans had rejected most of the medieval saints' days which had been holidays, but over time they developed a number of other occasions which were not exactly religious but which broke up the year: Armada Day, Guy Fawkes Day, Coronation Day, Oak Apple Day, the celebration of King Charles the Martyr. Puritans were naturally against these.

Many people know that during the Commonwealth period Christmas was suppressed, but it was not then the great feast that we have turned it into since the 1840s. Puritans would also have nothing to do with Ash Wednesday, Whitsun and Good Friday.

The Anglican Church courts were closed during the Civil War and Commonwealth. After they were re-established in 1660 they made very little attempt at general moral policing. The increasing number of dissenters were presented at Quarter Sessions. Those who wished to talk or write against the Church of England were fairly free to do so most of the time. When they overstepped the mark, it was nearly always because what they said was seditious or treasonable, not because it was 'heretical' or 'blasphemous'. For example, a lot of people felt strongly that the king should not be a Catholic.

Bishops were supposed to exercise supervisory powers over their clergy and there are many records of Bishops' Visitations. These mostly take the form of a questionnaire sent to some or all of the clergy in a diocese asking for a report on the religious state of the parish. For the most part they contain few names, but when ministers only had a few dissenters they might list them by name.

Most Nonconformist congregations had meetings of respectable members (often called elders) who discussed the behaviour of anyone whose name was brought to their attention. When they survive, the records can be full of anecdote and details of the relationships between husbands and wives, parents and children, employers and servants.

Meetings were not purely concerned with negative things. They dealt with 'clearness' for marriage (see below) and charitable help and support (of which there was often a great deal). The consistory (meeting of elders) records of Threadneedle Street (the most important Huguenot church in London) records the request of a deaf woman for permission to sit right under the pulpit within the communion rails. Naturally, they agreed.

There are a great many records of this sort for Quakers and Huguenots, who had central organizations to which records could be given when a church closed. The system must have worked the same way for a great many of the free-standing congregations, but far fewer of their records have survived.

The Anglicans had no parish system for policing behaviour, and records are more likely to relate to the positive and pleasant sides of life. Bell-ringing was very widespread and many churches or registers had records of who pealed the bells on particular occasions. Likewise there may be memorials recording those who had given money for the church or the poor. Other ceremonies, such as choir singing, beating the bounds or bonfires leave records occasionally.

Engagement and marriage

Marriage had originally been seen as a private contract between the parties. During the later Middle Ages a religious element intruded, and it was one of the important social planks of the Nonconformists that marriage was not a sacrament and not even a religious act. The Middle Ages had also accepted that a man and woman had every right to marry each other without telling anyone else that they were going to do it, and certainly without asking anyone's permission. The only problem was witnesses, but this was not a problem if both the man and woman agreed they were married. Thus in 1464 even the king (Edward IV) could be married to Elizabeth Woodville for six months without anyone knowing.

The concept that parents, or the wider family, must be consulted was fought over in the 16th century. At one end of the spectrum were those who said that children must never marry without their parents' consent, and that even middle-aged people with elderly parents must get permission. Others thought that 30 was probably a good age. In England the age below which consent was required was fixed at 21.

There was still no actual requirement to be married in public, or to give advance warning to anyone, or to have witnesses, or to be married in church. The Church of England (with a wide consensus of support) pushed for these things to be required, but they did not get their way until Lord Hardwicke's Marriage Act of 1753. Marriages elsewhere, or between under-age youngsters etc, were all legal before then – irregular, but not illegal – an important distinction.

Nonconformists to a greater or lesser extent held to the principle that marriage was not a religious act and that marriage in church was wrong. In England and Wales we know this most explicitly for Quakers since their records are best, but it was widely believed among the other Nonconformist groups. However, questions of illegitimacy and inheritance meant that many people were prepared to be 'sensible' against their preferences. In practice, we have no way of knowing how many people married outside the Church of England for reasons of religious principle.

During the first half of the 18th century an increasing number of people in London and the Home Counties were married by ministers in the Fleet Prison. These had taken over from the late 17th-century marriage shops at Holy Trinity, Minories, and St James's, Dukes Place. These were cheap and easy, but they were Anglican. The known records (which are extensive) are in the National Archives in RG 7.

A number of parishes elsewhere in the

country had vicars who attracted marriage trade from outside the parish. Entries should be in the ordinary parish register.

The principles of non-Anglicans are best seen by looking at the situation in Scotland where many 'marriage' entries are in fact announcements of engagement ('proclamation', in the phrase of the time). Presbyterians held to the old theology that a binding and proper marriage was produced by the first act of sexual intercourse after the couple declared their wish to take each other as husband and wife. Formally, this came to mean the first proclamation in church (what we would call the first calling of the banns). Many registers record that the couple were married a few weeks later – but others do not, or do not give the date, because the important thing was the proclamation.

We see the same in Huguenot records, where the registers are of 'Annonces et Mariages' and it is the engagement which is important. Once you were engaged you had to ask to be released and people could be sued for breach of promise (this was likely to be about money even if feelings played a part).

Quakers did not have the two stages. The couple stood up in the meeting and declared that they took each other as husband and wife. They did it before the whole congregation as a means of informing people and making sure that there were plenty of witnesses. It was not actually necessary to say the words in public, and there are many cases where we know that a couple were cleared for marriage but have no entry in the likely meeting registers.

We see best from Quaker and Huguenot records how much trouble the elders (women as well as men) took to establish that a man and woman were clear of other engagements, but the system worked the same for Presbyterians, Baptists and Separatists until 1753. After that, marriage was only legal if it had taken place in church after due formalities. Exception was made for Quakers, because they were so systematic, and for Jews, because they were not Christians. After 1753 many Catholics had two ceremonies and we often find two records of their marriage, sometimes on different days and possibly giving different information. Between 1754 and 1837 Nonconformists of all persuasions accepted the necessity to marry in the Anglican Church.

From July 1837 register offices were available for those who did not want a church wedding. These were aimed at Nonconformists, not at atheists, of whom there were very few. Marriages could take place in Nonconformist chapels in the presence of a registrar, but this was really aimed at providing a service for Methodists who very much believed in church marriage but were glad not to have to go to an Anglican church for it. By the mid-19th century a very high percentage of Welsh marriages were in register offices.

See *Using Marriage Records for Family Historians,* Pauline Litton (Federation of Family History Societies, 1996).

Divorce

There are, of course, two elements in divorce – the dissolution of a marriage and the right to enter into a new marriage. For those who believed in marriage as a sacrament or sort-of sacrament (the Anglican position was not at all clear-cut), remarriage was not possible while a former partner was living. Nor could a couple get a divorce without an Act of Parliament. They could obtain 'separation from bed and board', meaning that they no longer had to live or sleep together, and this solved the practical problem for some people. Even this was a lot of trouble, though, and not generally available for ordinary people.

Actions for divorce or separation were almost always scandalous since it was necessary to give reasons. Records of cases for separation may be in the church courts and the circumstances may be referred to in civil suits, but divorce cases had to be heard very publicly by Parliament. England really had no proper system of divorce until 1858, and even that remained fairly limited until after 1945.

Nonconformists had no problem with divorce in theory. Their view that marriage was a voluntary civil partnership naturally entailed the idea that the partnership could be ended voluntarily. If either party broke the terms of the marriage then the other party was entitled to compensation – but the marriage was over (unless the wronged party was prepared to continue with it). In practice, however, Nonconformists were subject to the law, which would not accept easy divorce or any form of remarriage.

Many couples separated unofficially and paired up with other people. This was often widely known and accepted in practice. The Anglican authorities were not likely to say or do much about it and the state authorities would not get involved either, so the level of acceptance was more or less dependent on public opinion. However, such partnerships were never legal.

Some people committed bigamy and there must have been many cases, especially in the towns, where this was unknown or ignored. Where cases came to court we may assume there was probably a particular reason (such as the 'proper' husband or wife making trouble). However, many first wives or husbands must have had no particular objection. The 'wife sales' highlighted by Thomas Hardy and often referred to actually represent a decent public attempt by two men to make it clear that they agree to the change and that in their terms neither they nor the woman are doing anything underhand. The 'sale' price represents a public acceptance that the first man has been compensated for the loss of his wife and the second man has agreed to take over financial responsibility for her.

Ordinations, appointments and licensing

Christianity has a long tradition of people being set aside for the service of God or their fellow Christians. Before the Reformation the Catholic Church had a basic division between priests (men), monks (men belonging to a religious order, for example, Benedictines,

Dominicans or Franciscans) and nuns (women, divided into choir sisters who prayed or praised God according to the style of their religious order and lay sisters who did the practical work of the convent).

There were other levels in the hierarchy of men. Lay brothers and deacons had not (yet) journeyed the whole way to priesthood; bishops, archbishops and some other less numerous ranks were priests who had climbed higher up the corporate ladder.

The Reformation rejected female religious of every sort, and it rejected the religious orders of men. It rejected the Pope, the head of the Catholics, but various denominations accepted more or less of the other hierarchies. Some accepted that priests were 'special' and had access (through the Apostolic Succession and ordination, another 'indelible mark on the soul') to powers that were not available to ordinary men. Others believed that all men were equal (the 'priesthood of all believers'), although godly wisdom and experience might be recognized as authoritative in practice.

Those who laid great stress on the special role of men set apart as intermediaries between God and Man called them priests and also tended to emphasize the things that went on at the altar. Those who emphasized equality tended to call their leaders ministers and to stress the power of Bible exposition and the sermon. In this book I have generally used the word minister because most priests did not seriously object to being called ministers, whereas many ministers did object to being called priests.

The Established (Anglican) Church was based on the parish, a geographical area with a parish church which all were supposed to attend and support, both religiously and financially. The minister appointed to run the parish was almost always either a rector or a vicar, and if he had any assistants they were called curates. Until the early 19th century it was not considered wrong for a man to be rector or vicar of more than one parish, and to draw all the salaries. If they were too far apart for him to perform the services in all of them it was perfectly permissible to appoint a curate who did the work – but for a lower salary.

None of this really mattered as far as our ordinary ancestors were concerned. What mattered were the personal qualities of the man who did the job, whatever his technical rank. The traditions of the Church of England allowed the parish clergy very wide freedom of belief and practice, and it is always worth seeing whether anything can be known of the beliefs and practices of the ministers who ran the parish where your ancestors lived. This will help you to picture what style of services they had and what sort of religion they preached. They are likely to have been very influential on our ancestors' thinking, and if our ancestors objected then it is useful to know what they were objecting to. It seems logical that if the Anglican clergyman's beliefs and practice chimed in closely with what Puritans or dissenters thought, then few people in his parish would feel conscientiously obliged to stay away.

Although ministers were technically appointed by the bishop or archbishop, the right to appoint (known as 'the gift of the living') lay in practice with many of the gentry. They were likely to appoint someone whose religious opinions they liked, all the more as they could not dismiss a man once they had appointed him. The records relating to Anglican ministers are well described in *My Ancestor was a Clergyman: How can I find out more about him?* by Peter Towey (Society of Genealogists, 2006).

Catholic clergy in the 16th and 17th centuries present a special problem since they were illegal and their careers were often fairly unstructured and hidden. Many used aliases so that they would not be recognized. However, many records of the early Catholic clergy have been published. Start with *English and Welsh Priests 1558–1800,* D.A. Bellenger (Downside, 1984) and *English and Welsh Priests 1801–1814,* C. Fitzgerald-Lombard (Downside, 1993). More detail appears in chapter 5 below.

Many of the Nonconformist congregations were much more democratic. They would invite a man to lead them and agree to pay his salary. If individuals fell out with him they were free to go elsewhere, and if enough of the congregation fell out with him they could dismiss him and appoint someone else. For most Nonconformists every congregation (every 'gathered community', they would have said) was independent of anyone else and free to do whatever it liked. In practice, they tended to share a shopping list of similar beliefs, but the only way to be certain of the angle any particular group took is to see whether its ministers published sermons or books – and read them.

All the Puritan clergy and many of the early dissenting clergy were Anglican ministers. In the 18th century there was no formal system of training for the dissenting ministry and in most congregations a man was a minister because other people recognized him as such. The Surman Index and other sources at Dr Williams's Library are the best way to find out what is known about a minister.

Dr Williams's Library, 14 Gordon Square, London WC1H 0AR is very important for the history of Baptists, Congregationalists and English Presbyterians in general (but it does not specialize in Methodists). It is emphatically *not* a first port of call for genealogy, and the register of births which was kept there between 1742 and 1837 is in the National Archives. However, it has long runs of the major denominational magazines, a great many histories of local meetings and lots of information on ministers. These will often shed light on the lives of ancestors you already know about. For a fuller account of the relevant material that the Library holds see the specialist books in the *My Ancestors were...* series listed in the bibliography.

Quakers had no formal system of ministers, but they did recognize the work of 'weighty friends' and came to call them ministers. The annual report to Yearly Meeting contained many Testimonies to Ministers Deceased, which usually give a short biography.

By the 19th century the main denominations had recognized clergy who were listed in the denomination's publications. Methodists were the most formally organized and many Presbyterian clergy came to England from Scotland or Northern Ireland where things were different. Baptists and Congregationalists had no authoritative centralized structure. Bible Colleges and training colleges developed, but any man of spiritual power could take a hall to preach in and establish an independent congregation.

Fortunately a great many ministers went into print. Apart from their wish to get involved in the questions of the day, they no doubt hoped to make some money. For the same reason many of them opened schools or took pupils into their homes.

Protestant ministers all had the option of marriage. Catholic priests (whether in an order or out in the world) took vows of celibacy. In our period this meant not only that they were not to marry, but also that they were not to have sexual relations. Many of us were brought up believing that these things were supposed to overlap (completely, if possible) and it is important to note that there are two distinct points of theology here and our ancestors saw them as (fairly) unconnected.

One point says that the best humans abstain from sexual relations because they take the mind away from God. If this attitude were universally followed then the human population would soon die out, but the early Christians were prepared to take that risk and in any case they only expected complete abstinence from the most godly, i.e. not very many people and even from them probably not all the time.

The second point relates to a man tying himself down with earthly responsibilities so that he cannot be available for any service God wants. This meant wife and children, but it could also mean parents and property. Thus the medieval church was not unbelievably shocked by priests who had women, and the general rule that priests' housekeepers must be above the age of 45 was because of a pragmatic acceptance that breaking the ideal vow of abstinence does not matter so much with women who are not going to have children. (Just a reminder that we have to try and understand our ancestors. It is not our business to decide if they were right or not.)

Two categories of people who were not ordained in any sense had to be examined for religious orthodoxy and licensed by the bishop. Schoolteachers (of whom England had very few compared to Scotland) were supposed to be Anglicans until the late 1600s. After Nonconformists gained religious freedom, this requirement naturally evaporated. Midwives, too, were supposed to be licensed since they would be baptizing babies who were likely to die and would have access to women at a time when they were psychologically vulnerable and of whom a certain percentage were also likely to die. The requirements on these groups really related to the time when the authorities were worried that a dying person might be baptized into the Catholic Church at the last minute, and this requirement also died away after the middle of the 17th century.

Swearing oaths

I am not referring here to insults and anger. Our ancestors had a range of religious and vulgar phrases intended to emphasize, insult or shock, extending from the mild and almost universally acceptable to the appalling and blasphemous, the fashion changing from generation to generation as it does with us.

I am thinking here of the reference to something holy to emphasize the truth of a statement or the seriousness of a promise or undertaking. In the Middle Ages people had tended to swear by saints or their relics or shrines but that fashion went out completely at the Reformation and people began to swear serious oaths on the Bible, or possibly the Gospels. This was pretty well universal and we see it most obviously in the oaths sworn in court before giving evidence ('to tell the truth, the whole truth and nothing but the truth') and in the standard phrase at the beginning of a will : 'In the Name of God, Amen.'

Many Nonconformists objected to this. On the one hand they had not yet developed the idea of the Bible as the unerring word of God (that idea reached its height in the 19th century as something of a reaction to Darwinism and archaeological excavations in the Holy Land). A lot of them really did not believe in any type of 'magic' and were uncomfortable using the word 'holy' about anything. The Quakers were probably furthest along this path, seeing the Bible as interesting and enormously valuable but not binding, since nothing is binding except what God has to say to us personally. Thus they saw swearing on the Bible as being no different in principle from swearing on the bones of a saint, which they were certainly not going to do.

The second aspect was the suggestion that

if on any particular occasion you swear to tell the truth you are giving people to understand that you do not always tell the truth. They were very straightforward about this and Quakers, being as so often at the far end of the spectrum, took a simple line: Let your Yea be Yea and your Nay be Nay. As we might say these days, they did not play games.

The refusal to swear oaths led Quakers in particular (but also others) into great difficulties. They were unable to give evidence in court, even in lawsuits where they were in the right, and they found themselves in contempt of court as soon as they were asked to swear that they would tell the truth. They were not able to swear the oath of loyalty to the monarch (though they were completely loyal). Thus many of them found themselves held in prison for months or even years, not because they had been found guilty and convicted but because their trials could not begin. This was a problem they could have solved but would not, and it was eventually solved by the authorities who invented the concept of affirming, to which Quakers found no objection.

Heresy, excommunication, disownment

Heresy sounds very grave, and the English-inherited mythology immediately associates it with Catholics, Bloody Mary and the Smithfield Fires. Unfortunately the Anglican Church burned a few heretics as well, for example Baptists who objected to infant baptism. Only a few – but how many is too many?

Excommunication, too, is seen as something Catholic and the majority of the records certainly relate to the Middle Ages. However, in the late 17th century quite a few dissenters, including Quakers, were excommunicated. There are formal records of this in the National Archives in C 85, C 207, CHES 38 and various KB series, with the last entry in 1880.

Excommunication had important consequences as regards ordinary life – you could not defend yourself in court, for example – and it could not simply be shrugged off if you did not believe in the church organization which had pronounced it.

Catholics were not excommunicated by the Church of England. It was *illegal* to be a Catholic and therefore the question of whether it might be immoral or heretical did not arise. Catholics who refused to attend the Church of England were known as recusants and are dealt with more fully below.

The various dissenting groups which

believed in formal membership all believed in dismissal from membership, though people with strong opinions were likely to jump before being pushed. Dissenters in England and Wales were never able to exercise the thoroughgoing control that they believed in. We have to look at Scotland to see what a society controlled by Presbyterians was like.

Quakers accepted the autonomy of the individual and would never instruct anybody what to believe. However, they believed that all right-thinking people would in practice believe the same and they often felt able to say that, as a group, they were not 'in unity' with people who believed something different or had gone counter to accepted practice. Such people would be disowned (the verb from disunity), but might well continue to attend under a cloud and were easily (sometimes very easily) accepted back if they gave sufficient evidence of being sorry.

Witchcraft and folk magic

There has always been a level of belief in folk superstition and in the various ways in which good and bad luck can be lost or won. Such beliefs are fairly innocuous as long they are the domain of the poor and uninfluential. However, they become very powerful when important people also believe in them, and between the end of the 15th century and the end of the 17th a great many middle and upper class people did believe in witchcraft – and those that did not had to be careful how they said so.

A great many people (more women than men, but not only women) were arraigned before the courts on the accusations of their neighbours and many of them suffered torture, imprisonment or death. Others were simply lynched locally. This was a Europe-wide phenomenon and the number of deaths per head of the population in this country was much less, for example, than in Scotland. Then, between about 1680 and 1700, people in power simply ceased to believe in witchcraft and no longer took accusations seriously.

In England research usually starts with records of the Quarter Sessions and the Assizes, either in the National Archives or in the county record offices or equivalent. Many records of Quarter Sessions have been catalogued and published.

Only one country in Europe was entirely free of persecutions for witchcraft – Spain. Most English-speaking people view the Spanish Inquisition through the eyes of Edgar Allan Poe and other writers of Gothic horror stories. It was established to root out heresy, but it was a court of law which followed the rules of evidence and found people innocent or guilty after due process, as the Americans say. It declared very early that it did not believe in witchcraft and that no accusations would be followed up. See *The European Witchcraft Craze*, H. Trevor-Roper (Penguin Books, 1967) and *Witch Hunting and Witch Trials*, C. L'Estrange Ewen (Kegan Paul, Trench Trubner and Co., 1929) which gives details of 1373 indictments in the Home Counties between 1559 and 1736.

Our ancestors had a wide range of beliefs which we do not treat as 'religious'. Many had to do with the presence of spirits which must be encouraged to help us or discouraged from hurting us. Others had to do with drawing down good luck or warding off bad luck. These attitudes, and the actions associated with them, have not left much of a paper trail, though one may see records of people touched for the 'King's Evil'.

Astrology and alchemy

Astrology underlay a lot of people's thinking, as did numerology. Then, as now, many people were aware of their star signs and the characteristics that were associated with them, and at some stage in their lives they would have had astrological charts drawn up – either by interested relatives (for example, when they were born) or as a means to understanding their illnesses and finding a cure. These may survive among family papers, but do not often get into the public domain. However, there are a number among the records of applications to the Civil Service (c.1855–1914) now at the Society of Genealogists.

The idea that the earth was the centre of the universe and that the sun, moon and planets revolve around it is obviously intuitive and needed a great deal of disproving. The influence of the stars on our lives and our futures also had a long history of general acceptance, and the Nativity story itself includes the Star in the East. You might disregard astrology, but as a Christian you could not utterly denounce it.

Alchemy, however, had no religious content. It was a serious attempt to develop chemical knowledge, and the suspicions of our ancestors derived from the fear that it might be involved with magic and witchcraft. It is simply a pity that so much of the work of 'alchemists' was focused on trying to turn ordinary metals into gold, something which we still do not think is possible. On the way up that blind alley, however, alchemists found out many other very valuable things.

Confession and penance

These were Catholic practices and in that church they were intended to be confidential. The Anglicans almost totally rejected the practice, though it was revived by High Anglicans and Anglo-Catholics in the 19th century. However, many of the dissenters believed very much in public confession of sins followed by public penance. Where consistory records or Quaker meeting records have survived, they often contain detailed evidence of what people were said to have done and the point at which they admitted their fault. The faults were often not so much religious as behavioural, eg drunkenness, since many dissenters had a clear view that bad behaviour showed that someone was not a proper Christian.

Catholics and Anglicans acknowledged that you could be a Christian who behaved badly, but dissenters were much more black and white over the issue. Proper Christians behaved properly, and therefore people who behaved badly were by definition not proper Christians.

Pilgrimages

This, too, had been very much a Catholic practice (and remained so). Anglicans rejected pilgrimages to shrines or holy places, but this did not go far enough for strict Puritans. The real theological problem came over graves, since Puritans who had thought it through said that going to visit a dead body was as bad as any other form of empty pilgrimage. This is one reason why burial records are so limited in Scotland (see *Burial and funerals* below).

Many English people made the Grand Tour of Europe and visited the great religious centres. However, they had the motives of tourists rather than pilgrims and many Protestants visited the great Catholic churches with every expectation of disapproving of the religion that they found there. The visitors' book of the English Hospice survives in Rome and tells us, for example, that John Milton visited Rome in 1638.

The Catholic shrines in England were all closed at the Reformation. However, 17th- and 18th-century Catholics continued to be aware of them, and there are records of Lancashire Catholics visiting Holywell in North Wales in the 1630s.

Anointing the sick

This does not have to do with death since it is supposed to do you good and help you heal. Anglicans did not emphasize the sacramental side of this, but most Christians felt that a visit from the minister when you were ill was a good thing (possibly with prayer, but without any actual anointing). That seems a rather unfocused way of putting it, but very few people would have wanted to define any formal good that it did while nevertheless finding it very acceptable and the sign of a good minister that he should do it. Visiting the sick was one of the 'corporal works of mercy' (to use the Catholic phrase) enjoined by the Bible. This rather contrasts with the practices of many modern Christians who take prayer for healing very seriously.

Last rites

This was a universal Catholic practice. We may assume it happened, or was wanted, for centuries after the Reformation, but there are no records of it until the 19th century, and very few then. However, Catholic priests were often called suddenly to a death bed and sometimes kept a note of where they had gone as a reminder of who had 'made a good death'. These include people whose relatives thought they were going to die, but who did not.

None of the Protestant churches had any formal ceremony of this sort.

Visitation of God

This phrase was fairly widely used to describe sudden or mysterious (but not suspicious) death and for most people it was probably something of an empty cliché when used in that sense. However, many people could not help taking satisfaction (from the highest religious motives) at the violent or unpleasant deaths (or any other tragedy) which befell people they disliked. Even Quakers (who tried to be charitable) often recorded that some informer was struck by lightning or that his wife ran off with a soldier, and there are many examples of this in Joseph Besse's *Sufferings of the People called Quakers for the Testimony of a Good Conscience*. Red-blooded ministers were not above calling down God's wrath on the people they thought deserved it.

The phrase appears from time to time on death certificates and as a verdict in coroners' inquests.

Burial and funerals

English family historians learn about Anglican

registers first and therefore think naturally in terms of baptism, marriage and burial registers as if these three life stages were automatically linked – but they are not. Those who have Scottish ancestry will know how many parish registers contain no (or few) entries for burials. Likewise for Catholics burial is not a sacrament, and there is no need for a priest to record when or where a burial took place. The point of burial is the hygienic and respectful disposal of the corpse and the reflections that the living make on the fact that we, too, must inevitably die some day. We meditate on the life of the dead person, as an example to copy or avoid.

Anglicans had the concept of holy ground – the area, usually round a church, where all baptized people would be buried. Ministers had the right to refuse burial to unbaptized people, or they might permit the burial without the service and possibly make a disparaging remark in the register. This would no doubt depend on the relations between the particular minister and the family of the deceased.

Nonconformists did not believe in the concept of holy ground, either for churches or burying. They were explicit that burials could take place anywhere and we have no way of knowing what percentage of Nonconformists were buried in their family's orchards or fields. Obviously this was only an option for country people, and in practice most Nonconformists brought their relatives' bodies to the churchyard. However, some Quakers established burying grounds of their own, and in London Bunhill Fields was established as a burying ground for all Nonconformists.

Almost all parents were Anglican and either had their children baptized or intended to. There are a few cases, often cited, where ministers refused to bury unbaptized children, and this sounds very hurtful to the feelings of the parents of the child. However, the minister's insistence that the child had gone to hell was intended to persuade the parents to have their other children baptized. Parents who believed in predestination knew perfectly well that their child had gone to hell. The Anglican minister believed that babies could be saved by baptism, and the Calvinist parents did not.

In fact, the difficulty arose at the point when Nonconformists were on the attack and asserting their right to be buried in the churchyard despite the fact that they were not Anglicans. In the end they established the principle that burial in the churchyard was for anyone who lived in the parish, regardless of their religious beliefs.

Catholics did not make any objection to burial in the Anglican churchyard since all the old churches had been Catholic ground originally. So far as we can see, the Catholic rites were performed at home and the family then accepted the Anglican rites without comment.

In fact, funerals were more a question of class than religion. Many people left detailed instructions, either privately or in their wills, but these were all about the number of carriages or mourners or how much money was to be given to poor people. Others stipulated a plain service, but as far as the religious content was concerned everyone had the same fundamental words of the Prayer Book service.

In England services were in the church or churchyard, which were usually in the same place. In Wales, Scotland and Ireland there were often traditional burying places which were not linked to a particular denomination. In parts of those countries it was not expected that women would go to funerals, but that was not the custom in England.

Until the late 18th century people did not expect to have permanent burial plots. They were put into the ground and in due course melted into the earth in a way that we find ecologically sound. A very, very small percentage of people might be preserved in tombs either inside or outside the church. The concept of a grave marker was therefore irrelevant.

Towards the end of the 18th century middle-class views changed; people began to want to mark the place where their relatives were buried and to bury other relatives in the same place. In country churchyards there was not much problem about assigning permanent spaces, but in the town churchyards this was almost impossible and led eventually to pressure for private cemeteries in the 1820s and 1830s and the purchase of big new parish cemeteries which were originally Anglican but quite a distance from the church. In 1853 an Act permitted the local authorities to open cemeteries which were not specifically Anglican, and many country parishes established an area which was not technically part of the churchyard.

See *Using Death and Burial Records for Family Historians*, Lilian Gibbens (Federation of Family History Societies, 1997).

Gravestones and inscriptions

Family historians often use these words as if

they were interchangeable, but they are not. A gravestone marks the actual place of burial. A memorial inscription (for example, on a wall) records something about the dead person, but without suggesting the body is buried there.

A monumental inscription may be either – the monument may be built over the dead person's burying place or it may be a statue or other marker recording the virtues of the deceased when the body is elsewhere or its whereabouts are not known. This is common for military or naval men or merchants who died a long way from home and whose bodies were disposed of where they died or were never found.

The distinction mattered very much to many of the Nonconformists. They made the point that the body was of no importance after the soul had left it and it was wrong to wish to mark it or pay any honour to it, let alone visit it, which was basically a pilgrimage. To put up a stone marking the whereabouts of a body showed that you thought there was something there worth marking. This was not so, and early Quakers required converts to take down any family gravestones now that they could see things rightly. However, there was no objection to remembering the dead, either

formally or informally, and therefore no objection to memorials. Thus the words 'In loving memory' were fine, but the words 'Here lieth the body' were not.

In the 19th century the old objection to gravestones withered away. Private cemeteries and the new borough cemeteries sold specific plots so that individual graves were clearly distinguished both on the ground and on the map in the office. There was also a highly developed trade in funereal monuments. This led to a new problem, especially in Scotland (where the objection to gravestones was much wider and more deeply rooted). As money became easier, many people erected gravestones to parents, grandparents, brothers and sisters and children who had died many years before. The dates (let alone the ages) may therefore be untrustworthy.

The problem was worse in Scotland because so many parishes had no burial registers and there was therefore no independent contemporary source with which to check a doubtful memory. In many cases you will never know that the ancient date on a gravestone is wrong, but in others there may be a discrepancy between dates on wills or leases or a statement that the man is dead when his son is apprenticed – or the date of remarriage of his wife. A contemporary gravestone is likely to be accurate, but stones that begin 'Erected by so-and-so in memory of' must be treated with care.

Many gravestones have quotations or Bible texts and these should always be noticed. Many are standard and may not reflect much personally on the dead person; others are more personal. However, to paraphrase Dr Johnson, no one has to tell the truth on a gravestone, and whatever people thought, or may even have said, very few people are prepared to carve negative truths in memorial inscriptions.

Wills, bequests and prayers for the dead

Family historians tend to concentrate on wills for the names of the relatives mentioned, but the first few lines show the testator thinking about his 'latter end' and are quite likely to show something of his religious beliefs.

Until the 19th century it was uncommon to make a will until the testator was dying and the only major exception to this were wills made in expectation of going on a long journey. Wills generally begin with a religious statement leaving the dying person's soul to

God, and this is often accompanied by a general statement of trust in 'the only merits of Jesus Christ' or some such phrase. These phrases may be standard form, inserted perhaps by the clerk or lawyer without any reference to the dying person's particular beliefs, but they should always be looked at in case there is anything more personal in them. The particular phrases used may show Puritan or Nonconformist beliefs (which were legal), but they are less likely to show Catholic or Unitarian beliefs since they were not legal. The testator's will then gives directions as to his burial and funeral (see above).

Many people left money to charity. In Catholic times many people had given money to the church to buy prayers for themselves or their dead relatives. They were buying a service that they wanted and many religious professionals lived on the income; however, any spare money left over went to relieve the poor.

After the establishment of Anglicanism prayers for the dead stopped, and people ceased to give money. There was a real problem in getting people to give money in return for – nothing. However, the custom grew of leaving money to the poor of the parish, either generally or in some specific way.

Anniversary masses and other services for the dead

These had been very common before the Reformation, but Protestants rejected the idea entirely. Catholics continued to want these, but as it was illegal to leave money 'for superstitious uses', they could not be explicit. However, there are many references in the wills of people who are known to have been Catholics which show that they have left private instructions. Examples include 'To Mr Challoner who knows my mind' or 'To Mr Dowey for purposes he knows of' – where Richard Challoner was the Catholic Vicar General of the London District, and Mr Dowey was not a person at all, but the Catholic college of Douai in France.

Many people like to do good in memory of the dead. This custom is probably more flourishing today than for hundreds of years as people name hospital wings after their wives or name Medical Research Trusts after their dead children.

Cornelius Walker of Southwark in the Parish of Saint Saviour Son of William Walker late of Kensington Park ... the County of Surry Grocer, Deceas'd, and Mary Key of Kinsham Street in London, Daughter of Robert Key late of Fulham London Hosier Deceas'd. —

Having declared their Intentions of taking each other in Marriage before several publick Meetings of the People of God called QUAKERS in London, according to the good Order used amongst them, whose Proceedings therein, after a deliberate Consideration thereof, were approved by the said Meetings; they appearing clear of all others, and having Consent of Parties and Relations concerned. Now these are to Certifie All whom it may concern, That for the full accomplishing of the said Intentions, this 31 day of the Fifth Month, called July, in the Year, according to the English Account, One Thousand Six Hundred and Ninety. They the said Cornelius and Mary Key appeared in a publick Assembly of the aforesaid People, and others, met together (for that end) in the publick Meeting-place at Gracemouth ... London and (according to the Example of the holy Men of God recorded in the Scriptures of Truth) in a solemn manner, he the said Cornelius Walker taking the said Mary Key by the Hand, did openly declare as followeth,

Friends In the fear of the Lord ... the presence of the People I take this my friend Mary Key to be my lawful married

And then and there in the said Assembly, the said Mary Key did in like manner declare as followeth,

Friends In the presence of the Lord and of you his People I take this my Loving friend Cornelius Walker to be my husband promising to be to him a Loving and faithfull wife ... Death separate us. —

And the said Cornelius Walker and Mary Key as a further Confirmation thereof, did then and there to these Presents set their Hands. And we whose Names are hereunto subscribed, being Present amongst others, at the solemnizing of their said Marriage and Subscription, in manner aforesaid, as Witnesses thereunto, have also to these Presents subscribed our Names, the Day and Year above-written.

Cornelius Walker
Mary Key

Dorothy Key
Mary Reeve
Eliz. Merriman
Abigail Merriman
Mary Rumph
Rigard Son
Mary Son

Ellen Bird
Sarah Gregory
Sarah Walkin
Grace Ellet
Sarah Taunton
Frances Urtick

Prudence Watts
Margaret Key
her O mark

Jno. E
Rich'd James Jun'r
Daniel Clare
W'm Clarkin
Benj. Anderby
Rich'd James Son
W'm Wood
G...

Henry Kirton
Tho. Maston
Tho. Bebb
Michael Rupert
Tho. Wayne
Joseph Wickeyn
Robert Veal
W'm Gunn...

Joseph French
W'm Tompson
David Newbury
John Zachary
W'm Masham
Joshua Wilson
G'r Harrison

Chapter 3

Denominations and their records

This book does not deal with religious genealogy before 1500. Medieval genealogy is often possible, but religious records are not the prime sources. Manumissions, however, are a source which is not well known, and we may stretch a point by including them here. Many of our ancestors were tied to the land as serfs, but social circumstances changed in the 15th century and large numbers of them were released. Many examples of this survive in the records of medieval estates, and they naturally give the names of all the members of the family who were being freed.

The medieval church was an enormous landowner, however – and so were the universities which were as much religious institutions as the great monasteries and convents. A great many of their records survive, little used by family historians, but they are not religious records in the sense with which this book is concerned. For the wonderful personal detail that can be found in the records of religious institutions, see *The Common Stream* by Rowland Parker. This relates to the village of Foxton, Cambridgeshire, much of which belonged over centuries to the Abbess of St Albans. However, to repeat the point, these are not religious records.

At diocesan level the church courts functioned and have extensive records in which our ancestors may appear with genealogical detail. There was a policy against marriages between cousins up to the seventh degree, but I imagine this must have been more honoured in the breach than the observance. It presumably produced a steady stream of small payments for a licence for those within the prohibited degrees to marry anyway.

The church courts were concerned with immorality, witchcraft and heresy, and we may profit genealogically from what may have been very unpleasant experiences for our ancestors. The detailed records of the beliefs of a number of East Anglian Lollards have been published and show us that many of the mainstream Puritan beliefs of the 16th and 17th centuries go back to at least the early 15th century:

'The sacrament of Baptem doon in water in forme costumed in the Churche is nother necessarie ne vailable to mannys salvacion.'

'Only consent betuxe man and woman, with consent of the frendys of bothe parties, suffiseth for matrimony, withoute expressing of wordis or solemnizacion in churche.'

'It is as meritorie and as medful and as profitable to all Cristis peple to be byryed in myddynges, medues or in the wilde feldes as it is to be byryed in churches or churcheyerdes.'

'No maner of pilgrimage oweth to be doo to ony places of seyntes but only to pore peple.'

See *Norwich Heresy Trials 1428–1431*, ed. Norman P. Tanner (Camden Fourth Series, 1977) and – a hundred years later – *Kent Heresy Proceedings 1511–12*, ed. Norman Tanner (Kent Archaeological Society, vol. 26, 1997). The names of those brought before the court are given, with their parish of residence.

Excommunication had legal and financial consequences as well as religious ones, and significations of excommunications from 1220 are in the National Archives, in C 85. They give details of residence, occupation, paternity and offence, and are in Latin. Those from the reign of Elizabeth I to that of Queen Victoria are in C 207 with a card index by diocese. Enrolments of writs to enforce excommunications are on the Controlment Rolls 1330–1843, in KB 29 and 1844–80 in KB 5. Subsequent proceedings are in the Coram Rege Rolls 1272–1701 in KB 27 and the Plea Rolls 1702–1911 in KB 28.

Separate material for Cheshire appears in CHES 38.

At parish level survivals are unsystematic, but there are sometimes lists of those who left bequests to the church, particularly those who left money for masses to be said for the benefit of their souls or those of their relatives. These sometimes provided for the building of a special chapel (a chantry) and the employment of a chantry priest. These were surveyed by the Crown Commissioners in 1545 and 1547. Any land held for this use was confiscated in 1547 by the Court of Augmentations. See E 300, 309, 310, 311, 312, 315, 321, 403; SC 2 and SC 12.

The medieval church also had a wide range of guilds and societies, often connected with some particular saint or relic, and there are numbers of membership lists of these. See *The Stripping of the Altars* for an account of the changes in London and *The Voices of Morebath* (both by Eamon Duffy) for an account of how the pendulum swung back and forth in one moorland Devon village.

There are extensive records of clergy and religious of all sorts, and detailed biographies can be built up for individuals whom it may be possible to link using non-religious sources. However, the records' usefulness for genealogy is limited by the policy that religious professionals should not have wives and children.

The dissolution of the monasteries is very well documented. The lands were confiscated, but the monks and nuns were given pensions and these were paid at least until the 1570s. The pension lists record what jobs the men had taken and whether the women had married. Incidentally, the Catholic clergy were all released from their vows of celibacy in 1547 – so it is possible to be descended legitimately from monks and nuns of the period.

See 'The Dissolution of the Monasteries and Chantries: Sources in the National Archives', Aidan Lawes (*Genealogists' Magazine*, vol. 27, no. 11, September 2003) and 'The State of the

Ex-Religious and Former Chantry Priests in the Diocese of Lincoln 1547–1574', G. Hodgett (Lincoln Record Society, vol. 53, 1959). The biographies of all ex-religious in Yorkshire have been published by Yorkshire Archaeological Society (vol. 150) and a database of priests and former monks and nuns is being compiled.

The Anglican church after the Reformation

The English National Church was established to be exactly that – a way for English people to worship God, led by their monarch. This took over from the concept of a universal church headed by the Pope and of which everyone was a part, regardless of their nationality.

In the 16th century this was a development throughout the Christian world and was just one aspect of the establishment of increasingly centralized national states. Similar churches were established in the Scandinavian countries, and in 1555 the Treaty of Augsburg (which brought a couple of generations of peace to the warring religious groups of Germany) established the principle that subjects must be of the same religion as their ruler.

In fact, the same principle applied more or less in Catholic countries. King Philip of Spain was devout and loyal to the Papacy, but he exercised the same sort of control over the Church in Spain as Henry VIII – and more than Elizabeth I. A hundred years later Louis XIV also controlled the Church in France through the appointment of bishops.

The same principle also obtained in Eastern Europe. Here the Orthodox Church was almost universal, but the Russian Orthodox Church was for Russians and the Greek Orthodox Church was for Greeks, and so on.

Underlying that principle was another: that everyone was a Christian. They should both worship and behave in the right way, but their rulers (both civil and religious) had the authority to tell them what that was. It was their ruler's duty to make sure they got into heaven and the subjects' to do what they were told.

Church attendance was a community activity and the services were a corporate act of worship. There was no need for the ordinary Christian to try for a private road to God.

However, the Anglican Church contained a spectrum of beliefs from the almost-Catholic to the very Puritan. People held diametrically opposing viewpoints. For the sake of solidarity Elizabeth I developed a form of liturgy which was fairly acceptable to everyone, and allowed those who really minded to alter even that.

Ministers in their own churches had a wide range of choices while their congregations could agree or disagree, think anything and say almost anything about it – provided they obeyed the law and attended.

Such flexible inclusiveness has always been the great strength of the Church of England. The centre is always trying to hold against the efforts of those who are so confident they are right that they want to make everyone else say or do it their way.

By the mid-17th century, and certainly by the early 18th century, very large numbers of people in the towns had ceased to come to church regularly. They came when they wanted to – and a very high proportion of the population showed up for the important life events detailed in the previous chapter. However, they often did not come in between.

From the mid-19th century it was common for children to go to Sunday school and/or even church when their parents did not go. There also grew up a range of activities, more or less religious – Girl Guides, Boy Scouts, Pathfinders – which brought the children into contact with Christian morality.

This situation continued pretty well until the middle of the 20th century. People were baptized, married and buried in church. They learned their Christianity and Bible knowledge at school and Sunday school. They accepted public worship at school, in the army and on all public occasions. People of other denominations sneered at this form of religion and said very often and very explicitly that it was not good enough, but it appears to have served the majority well – and it still suits a surprisingly high percentage of the population today.

The basic administrative structure of the church was the parish, an area served by a parish church. People were not really supposed to go a parish church outside their area since that undermined the sense of community. Certainly people were not to be baptized, married or buried in other churches. This situation weakened a little in the 19th and 20th centuries, but it remained necessary to make the case for baptism or marriage somewhere else. The question of burial was different after 1853 since a high proportion of people were buried in public cemeteries – people who did not have a church commitment of their own would accept the services of the duty minister, any of the local ministers on the rota.

Parish registers of baptisms, marriages and burials were ordered to be kept from 1538.

About 10 per cent of them survive from this early date and about another 10 per cent from 1558. Marriage licences were issued by the Bishop in each diocese and wills were proved in the Bishop's Court. Gravestones were not common until after 1750 or even later; inscriptions on gravestones in country churchyards have often been transcribed and even published. The survival rate of those in town churchyards is much lower, but they, too, have often been copied. The chances of survival in borough cemeteries (after 1853) are much higher, but inscriptions from very few large cemeteries have been copied.

Parish registers record the baptisms, marriages and burials of all Anglicans. In practice, many Nonconformists also appear, particularly in the marriages and burials. Parish registers were instituted in 1538 and are our prime source for family history until the mid-19th century. Almost all of them have now been deposited in county record offices or local equivalents. A great many have been microfilmed and are available through the Mormons. Very many have been transcribed, indexed and/or published – but many have not, and searches can still sometimes take a long time. Many early registers are in Latin.

All mainstream books on family history describe their format and there is not space to go into that detail here. This book is more concerned with the logic behind the records, how they can be accessed and how they can help family historians.

Most other 'parish records' in fact concern the parish as chief administrative unit for local government. The records of rates and the administration of the Poor Law are often large, but have no religious content. Poor relief was given out to any parishioner who needed it, regardless of religious opinions. Likewise Nonconformists had no objection to paying their rates to the parish administration. Religion and local government were clearly distinguished by everyone.

Other Protestant denominations

The other denominations were always a minority. Even taken altogether they never constituted five per cent of the population (although by the 19th century they were a much higher percentage than that of church-goers). However, they generally consisted of committed people who felt that the Anglican Church had got it wrong in a number of ways. They were stronger in some areas than others, generally speaking in the North and in East Anglia. In the time of Wesley and in the 1840s Nonconformity spread strongly among the 'unchurched' and people speak of groups such as the Cornish tin miners. However, the visibility and commitment of Nonconformists were always out of proportion to their numbers.

I had originally written 'felt strongly', but this book is for family historians and we should not picture our specific ancestors as deeply committed unless we know they were from actual evidence. As time went by, Nonconformists included many people who had simply grown up in their particular style of belief and worship and did what they did because they had always done it. You do not have to believe 'strongly' when you are not in opposition to anyone else.

This is particularly true in the 19th century when many people attended a church which was nearby or socially remunerative, and the theological and liturgical differences between many of the denominations died away.

However, many people had a general approach and looked for churches and ministers which matched that. Those who believed in the importance of the sacraments, ceremonial and church authority are usually called 'High' Anglicans. Those who emphasized plainness, sermons and the (more or less) equality of all believers are called 'Low' Anglicans. By the 19th century Low Church Anglicans were not very different from most types of Nonconformist. Both groups were often called evangelical, but this description was not used much before 1800. It implies concentrating on the gospels and the 'good news' of salvation. It came to mean Low Church Christians who took seriously the business of converting non-believers (or wrong-believers) to Christianity.

Until the late 19th century Nonconformists were almost wholly lower middle class. Even those at the top end of the working class were helped into the middle classes by the very fact of being Nonconformists. In terms of those above them, this is partly because the upper middle class and upper classes were able to influence the church in their own parishes and therefore had little need to leave it; partly because many middle- and upper-class careers required an Anglican communion certificate. However, many Anglicans of good class had Low Church beliefs.

Economic circumstances excluded many lower down the social scale from Noncomformist religions. The essence of Noncomformist practice was private Bible reading and if you could not read (or did not have someone to read to you daily), then you could not easily be a Nonconformist. You also needed a chair and a fire and a little space and enough energy after the day's work, and enough education to think about what you read. Lots of labourers did not possess those things.

During the 19th century the ability to read and the money to have a chair and a candle and a fire became more and more common among the working classes – so therefore did Nonconformity.

Puritans

Puritans were members of the Church of England between 1559 and 1642. They thought it had not been sufficiently purified of Catholic doctrine and practice, but they had made a policy decision to stay inside the Church and change it. They shared a general list of beliefs which emphasized the pulpit rather than the altar, sermons rather than cere-monial, improvised prayers rather than set prayers. There were other important issues where they did not agree, above all on the concept of authority and on the question of whether everybody could be saved if they believed the right things (Arminianism) or whether salvation was a decision of God's regardless of the individual (Calvinism).

In practice, these points were worked out by thoughtful individuals – many of whom were Church of England ministers giving sermons and writing tracts to support their thinking. Almost nobody was outside the Anglican Church in this period and even Catholics and members of the foreign churches were half in/half out. There are no genealogical records of Nonconformists before the Civil War because there were no separate Nonconformists before the Civil War. This includes the Pilgrim Fathers who were Church of England, however much they disapproved of it. (Please do not write to me about the minuscule number of famous individuals of whom that is not true. Even their marriages, burials and wills will be found in the Church of England system.)

The only exceptions were the French- and Dutch-speaking churches which were given permission to hold services in their own languages. These were non-parochial and non-Anglican, but they were not in opposition to the Anglican Church that licensed them. The various Catholic countries also maintained embassy chapels which were not illegal.

Queen Anne, wife of James I, and Queen Henrietta Maria, wife of Charles I, also had Catholic services in the royal palaces under the terms of their marriage settlements – but these, of course, were not Puritan.

Life became difficult for Puritans after 1633 when Archbishop Laud began to tighten up on the rules, but in practice they all obeyed and continued to attend their parish church. It was the Scots' refusal to obey which originally triggered the Civil War.

The Civil War

With the outbreak of the Civil War three groups proceeded to establish themselves very quickly: Presbyterians, Congregationalists and Baptists. They did not agree with each other, either over church forms or religious beliefs, but they usually united when it came to opposing Anglicanism.

Presbyterians

This group believed in the authority of ministers (but not bishops). They were the state church in Scotland and we see there how a Presbyterian church might have worked out in England if it had ever been in control. Presbyterians were in charge in England for a short period after 1648, but they were never able to control the other Nonconformists of the period, let alone the Anglicans.

Presbyterianism is really a form of church government rather than a set of beliefs, though they were almost all Calvinists. They believed that the religious authorities were superior to the state, and that if people did misbehave the Church should be able to call on the state to punish them.

Congregationalists

Here, too, the chief point is the form of church government. Congregationalists (also known as Separatists or Independents) believed that the godly (who were always going to be few in number) would want to come together and form groups, but that they were all basically equal. The group might recognize the spiritual power of some individual and invite him to be their minister, but the bottom line was always that the group employed the minister and could send him away if they did not like his style.

During the Civil War, Presbyterians dominated Parliament, but Congregationalists came to dominate the Army. In the late 1640s and 1650s they steadily took over, but they had no workable theory of how to govern a country;

England was in practice a military dictatorship.

Baptists
People who objected to infant baptism really concentrated on that issue. They were also known as Anti-Baptists, Anabaptists and Antipaedobaptists, but none of those names stuck. The word Anabaptist was often used by their enemies since it brought back memories of a 16th-century German group who had fallen into anarchy and were a scandalous memory.

Baptists might have any form of church government and any of the other Puritan beliefs. In particular they were divided into General Baptists (who were Arminian), Particular Baptists (who were Calvinists) and Strict Baptists (who would not let anyone receive communion who had not been baptized as an adult). One point brought them together: opposition to infant baptism.

The records of these three groups are scanty. A small number of baptism registers are in the National Archives, in RG 4. There must have been many others, but few are known. The Baptists, of course, did not practice infant baptism.

As regards marriages, the Commonwealth instituted a form of civil marriage performed by registrars who appear to have used the parish registers to record these. The system lasted from 1653 to 1660. They were generally settled in the larger towns rather than in every small parish. Most Nonconformists found these acceptable (the Quakers did not), and so many entries which are in an Anglican register were non-religious in spirit.

During the Civil War and Commonwealth people were free to bury their dead 'in the middens or the meadows or the wild fields' rather than in the parish churchyard, but there is not much evidence that many did so.

For more detail on the background to these groups, see *Sources for the History of English Nonconformity 1660–1830*, Michael Mullett (British Records Association, 1991); *English Nonconformity for Family Historians*, Michael Gandy (Federation of Family History Societies, 1998); 'Sources for Nonconformist Genealogy and Family History', D.J. Steel (National Index of Parish Registers, vol. 2, 1973).

Quakers

Quakers were a completely new group which began in the early 1650s and expanded dramatically. They did not believe in any form of church government, or liturgy, or ministry. In the 1650s they were very radical, and many of them were confident that the world was about to end. After 1660 they accepted that this was not going to happen straightaway and developed longer-term systems.

Quakers have a reputation for excellent record-keeping. Partly this is based on their effectiveness in conserving the records of meetings which had closed. We may suppose that many free-standing Presbyterian, Congregational and Baptist meetings had equally good records at the time, but had no one to hand them on to when the meeting closed. On the other hand Quakers, having more extreme opinions than the other groups, particularly in their strong witness against church marriage under any circumstances, had more of an interest in recording the marriages they themselves witnessed. Moreover, as they had no ministers and the meetings really were overseen by other meetings, the secretaries ('clerks') soon developed the habit of keeping detailed minutes to be agreed on the spot.

As regards records of births, marriages and deaths, many Quaker meetings began to keep these in the 1650s. However, it was not until 1669 that George Fox positively enjoined it, with the result that many meetings which have good records from then on have nothing for the first 15 years.

Quaker records of marriage are particularly valuable since it was common practice for everyone present to sign the certificate as a witness.

The Meeting Books of many local meetings have survived. At the most local level there were often separate Men's Meetings and Women's Meetings. There was then a hierarchy of Preparative Meetings (purely local), Monthly Meetings (local), Quarterly Meetings (area wide) and Yearly Meetings (nationwide). Quakers were very thoroughly organized.

Quakers gave particular offence by their doctrine of equality, refusing to take their hats off in the presence of gentry or to use respectful turns of phrase. They suffered a great deal of persecution for their refusal to attend Anglican services and for holding services of their own. These could be particularly annoying as the magistrates wanted to prosecute them for using seditious language – but many Quaker meetings were held in complete silence. Quakers were also frequently sued for non-payment of tithes and held in prison for refusing to swear oaths.

Fortunately for us, Quakers recorded all these incidents of persecution, and not only at local level. London Yearly Meeting received accounts from the counties of everything Quakers had suffered and these were written up year by year in the Great Books of Sufferings. The most interesting of these were extracted by Joseph Besse and published in 1752 as *Sufferings of the People Called Quakers for the Testimony of a Good Conscience*. This is being reprinted by the Quaker publisher, Sessions of York.

Quakers were almost always a step beyond the other types of Nonconformist. They objected to the use of heathen names for the days and months and invented the system of referring to them by numbers. Thus their records will refer to a birth on the 14th of the 9th in a way that we understand.

Not completely, however. Until 1752 the New Year began on March 25th and March was the first month of the year. A birth on the 14th of the 9th is therefore referring to November.

For a more detailed account of the records of Quakers see *My Ancestors were Quakers*, Edward Milligan and Malcolm Thomas (Society of Genealogists, 1983).

Muggletonians
These followed a charismatic leader, Lodowick

Did you know?
Quakers did not approve of using the names for months (or days) which derived from the old Roman gods, and they became the first people to use the numbering system, e.g. the 4th of the 12th 1703. However, this can lead us to make mistakes as, until 1752, March was the first month and therefore the 12th month was February.

Before 1752 Quakers had no objection to using September, October, November and December because these actually were the 7th, 8th, 9th and 10th months. After 1752 this was no longer true as they had become the 9th, 10th, 11th and 12th months, and Quakers would not use them.

Muggleton. They were never very numerous, but they survived the Civil War and went on as a very small group until the 20th century. Their archive is now in the British Library.

Episcopalians
This group appears a great deal in Scottish history. They believed in the role of bishops in authority over local ministers. This ran counter to the doctrine of the Presbyterians who had control in Scotland, but in England the Church of England had bishops so was Episcopalian. During the Civil War and Commonwealth those who supported bishops were out of power, but it is not usual to call them

Episcopalians. We still call them Anglicans (or royalists, since the two positions overlapped).

Other groups in the Civil War

In the freedom (some said chaos) of the 1640s and 1650s, many individuals and small groups looked for God. Many of them developed beliefs along the same lines and are called either Seekers or Ranters, but this does not imply that they were organized. Smaller groups included Diggers and Fifth Monarchy Men, but this was a time of highly developed individualism.

From the family history point of view, many of these groups kept no records themselves. Their marriages and burials may or may not be traceable in some formal, probably Anglican, record, but we are pretty unlikely to find any record of the births of their children. Many of them did not believe in baptizing.

After the Civil War

After the Restoration in 1660 and the Act of Uniformity in 1662, Presbyterians, Congregationalists and Baptists were placed under heavy pressure. I do not wish to say persecuted because we must keep a sense of perspective and the majority of our ordinary ancestors were merely presented at Quarter Sessions and fined for non-attendance at church. Quakers were sued for non-payment of tithes, but the other Nonconformist groups did not take that stand. Worse things happened to a few leaders but imprisonment, which was fairly widespread, was self-imposed by the individual's conscience. The authorities would have let most of them go if they would only have complied on points which seemed pretty unimportant to everyone else.

After 1689 Nonconformists had freedom of worship. They flourished initially, and by 1715 there are thought to have been about 550 Presbyterian congregations, 300 Independent and 250 Baptist with about 250,000 attenders. However, their numbers declined by about 50 per cent over the next 50 years and might well have sunk further if it had not been for the general inspiration of the Wesley brothers and George Whitefield.

Actually, it was too late for English Presbyterians. They had mostly drifted into the 18th-century view of God as 'the great clockmaker in the sky' and had more or less become Unitarians. After a significant court case some of their charitable monies were taken away from them on the grounds that they no longer held the beliefs for which they had been given the money.

Congregationalists and Baptists began to rise in numbers on the back of Methodism. They remained significant in numbers throughout the 19th and early 20th centuries, but in terms of power and influence they were always in the shadow of the Methodists.

Unitarians
Unitarians did not believe in the Trinity. They accepted the Godship of the Father, but not of the Son or the Holy Spirit. They remained illegal until 1813 and could not present themselves as a religion at all, instead calling themselves Societies. They were few in number but articulate, literate and influential.

A great many Presbyterian meetings developed Unitarian beliefs. See *My Ancestors were English Presbyterians/Unitarians*, Alan Ruston (Society of Genealogists, 1993).

Moravians
The Moravian Church had a long history in central Europe and was in the mainstream of Calvinist churches. The Moravians suffered greatly during the Thirty Years' War and by the early 1700s were worshipping as

Did you know?

Until 1752 the New Year began on 25 March. This was the beginning of the Christian Era, that is, nine months before the birth of Christ. Thus, for example, we say that Charles I was executed on 30 January 1649, but at the time, and for a hundred years after, the date was known as 30 January 1648. In transcribing registers or writing up our family histories, we should always adapt the date from 'Old Style' to 'New Style'.

Long before 1752 several European countries had changed to having New Year's Day on 1 January, and many English people were aware of this. We often find a system of 'double dating' in old records, e.g. 30 January 1648/9, and modern family historians often use this as well. It does not mean you are not sure of the year, but that we give the year a different number from the one it had at the time.

In using indexes always check whether the date has been copied unchanged from the record source or altered to the modern form. Otherwise it can appear, for example, that two babies were born less than nine months apart, or that the mother was buried many months before her last child was baptized!

Lutherans, a group with no obvious counterpart in England but probably best represented by the Anglicans. In the 1720s they became well known for their 'settlements' and their missionary work, especially under the protection of Count von Zinzendorf.

The first Moravians came to England in

1723. In 1735 missionaries travelling to Georgia fell in with John Wesley and greatly influenced him. Wesley visited their settlement at Herrnhut in Bohemia, but Moravian work in England continued separately from the growth of Methodism. However, like Wesley, they were interested in changing people's perceptions rather than their denomination, and many people who became Moravians also remained whatever they had been before. By 1747 they had 1,000 members in Wiltshire and 1,200 in Yorkshire. By 1800 there were about two dozen congregations with about 5,000 members but with many more attenders and hearers. Moravians' numbers probably never exceeded this in the 19th century, but there was and is a very substantial body of Moravians in the USA.

For an excellent account of the records see *National Index of Parish Registers*, vol. II, D.J. Steel (Society of Genealogists, 1973).

Sandemanians
Robert Sandeman, under the influence of John Glas who later became his father-in-law, held extreme views on the doctrine of justification by faith. His career was spent mostly in Scotland and America, but he founded a

church in London in 1760 and there were others at Liverpool, Newcastle-upon-Tyne, Nottingham and Whitehaven. In Wales there were Sandemanian churches at Swansea, Carmarthen, Llangadock and Llangyfelach.

Inghamites

Benjamin Ingham was an Anglican vicar and initially a companion of John Wesley. He, too, was associated with the Moravians, but then founded an organization of his own which was Calvinist and broke away from the Anglican Church in 1755 by ordaining his own ministers. Inghamite societies continued to flourish for a couple of generations after his death in 1772, but numbers gradually drifted down in the course of the 19th century. There are some registers in the National Archives in series RG 4.

New Jerusalemites (or Swedenborgians)

Emmanuel Swedenborg inspired followers, but did not either preach or found a church himself. He believed that the spiritual and physical worlds were parallel and that one could live in both. His outlook was Unitarian, and he died in 1772.

In 1784 followers founded the New Church and the first congregations met in London

(1788) and Birmingham (1791). A couple of Anglican ministers popularized the movement in Lancashire. By the 1851 religious census there were 50 Swedenborgian places of worship and 4,846 people attended the services. Registers are in the National Archives in series RG 4.

Universalists
Various religious groups and individuals have believed that, in the end, everyone will be saved. There were early 19th-century Universalist churches in Plymouth, Devonport, Portsmouth and (in 1851) London. No registers are known for them but the Rev. David Thom of Liverpool deposited his register in what is now series RG 4.

Key Nonconformist records (17th and 18th centuries)
As regards records, there are many registers of baptism in the National Archives in series RG 4–8, but only two registers of marriages and very few registers of burials. Baptisms and marriages have been microfilmed and have been on the Mormon FamilySearch website for 30 years; they are now also available online. Every time you look at that, you see all there is.

In 1742 the London dissenters established a register at Dr Williams's Library for the registration of their births. They hoped to persuade the courts to treat this as legal evidence, but were unsuccessful until 1836 when all Nonconformist registers got recognition.

The vast majority of Nonconformist marriages almost certainly took place in the Anglican Church – but we cannot be certain since the Anglican registers themselves have not all survived. After 1753 this was certainly the case. Between 1754 and 1837 all marriages had to be in the Church of England, except for those of Quakers and Jews. The Nonconformists all complied with this.

Burials, too, are almost wholly in the Church of England registers. Thus the sign of a Nonconformist family – if we are meeting them for the first time – is a parish register which contains marriages and burials for a family but few or no baptisms.

In the years 1662 to 1689 many Nonconformists were presented at Quarter Sessions, with or without a description of their denomination. After 1689 they were free to worship and from 1691 they were free to register buildings for worship. These registrations, originally in the records of Quarter Sessions, are also in

RG 31 at the National Archives covering the years 1691–1853. They highlight how many records may not have survived since they refer to thousands of meetings registered for worship, when we only have a few hundreds of registers in series RG 4.

Since Nonconformists were mostly people of respectable life they are likely to appear in all the records of the middle class, particularly the records of land and trade. We may be able to document their marriage and burials and their lives – but have to go without any exact entry of their births.

Methodists

John and George Wesley and George Whitefield began their work in the 1730s and intended to preach a new spirit of Christian life and worship to people who they thought were largely formalists – emphasizing community acts of worship. Formalism was not then as strong a criticism as it would be now. Almost everyone believed in God and expected that he had expectations about the individual's beliefs and behaviour. The Quakers had believed that God would deal directly with the individual if he had any message, but not that he would do so all the time. It was Wesley who first popularized the concept of a 'personal' God with whom we have a two-way relationship.

Wesley and Whitefield parted company fairly early as Whitefield was a Calvinist (salvation for the chosen) and the Wesleys were Arminian (salvation for all who wanted it). Their preaching was intended to revive the Church of England and was very successful. It was almost an accident that Methodists parted company with the Church of England in 1787 as there was nothing in their beliefs or forms of worship which made that necessary. Certainly much of their 'enthusiasm' (a word of very strong criticism in the 1700s) was distasteful to more restrained people, but the tide was moving their way and despite the separation there was very little to distinguish Methodists from Low Church Anglicans – except that Methodists were almost wholly lower middle class.

As soon as Wesley died, Methodists broke up into groups. Apart from the Methodists there were the Methodist New Connexion (1797), Primitive Methodists (1807), Bible Christians (1815), Protestant Methodists (1827), the Wesleyan Methodist Association (1836) and the Wesleyan Methodists (1849). The

Protestant Methodists and the Wesleyan Methodist Association joined to form the United Methodist Free Churches in 1857; some of the others joined together in 1907 and most of the rest in 1932. It all mattered very much to those involved.

Many early Methodists were quite happy to attend both Anglican services and their own, but this flexibility rather withered as a generation grew up which had only known Methodism.

Methodists did not believe in membership in the same strict way as the older forms of Nonconformity. Nevertheless their chapels had to be paid for.

See *My Ancestors were Methodists*, William Leary (Society of Genealogists, 1999).

Methodist birth and baptism records
Once they had left the Church of England and become Nonconformists, Methodists dominated Nonconformist numbers and took the lead in Nonconformist politics. The Wesleyans had no commitment to the anti-Anglican theological points which had been so important to Puritans, Presbyterians, Congregationalists and Baptists, and were therefore vital to the development of the general one-size-fits-most form of Low Church evangelical Christianity

which became very widespread by the mid-19th century.

Since Methodists came directly out of the Church of England without any fundamental theological or liturgical dispute, they quickly established a system for recording infant baptisms. Their records after 1787 thus constitute a high proportion of the non-parochial registers which are at the National Archives in series RG 4. Their marriages and most of their burials took place in the Church of England.

Methodist influence caused most other congregations to consider their position as regards baptismal registers. The general development of the campaign to obtain legal recognition of non-Anglican registers began to persuade even Baptists to keep records of births, something which had no conceivable religious purpose. Many Baptist chapels have birth registers from the early 1800s.

The Wesleyan Methodists established a registry of births in 1817, hoping to provide a system of trustworthy birth certificates parallel to that found at Dr Williams's Library (page 73). The registers can be viewed in the National Archives, and the entries are on the Mormon FamilySearch website.

Later denominations

There were and are a number of later denominations which were numerically important in the 19th century. However, from 1837 their records are not the place to start when building a family tree. They all complied with the system of registering births and deaths and after 1853 their burials, perhaps with gravestones, will be in the borough cemetery. Some of them conducted marriages, at which the registrar attended until 1898, and many ministers were then licensed for the independent conduct of marriage ceremonies. Others did not, and their members' marriages will be at the State Registry Offices or in some other denomination. They all appear in the 10 year censuses, proved their wills in the state system after 1858 and appear in the other standard records of the 19th century.

The chief reasons for using the marriage and infant baptism registers (if any) of the various denominations are to save money on GRO certificates and to browse for related entries helping us to build up a picture of which relatives attended the same meetings as our direct ancestors, and over what period. This is very useful.

Other, not purely genealogical, records can

be interesting in showing aspects of the personal lives of individuals, particularly as regards membership, degree of participation in what the congregation was doing, both religious and social, and disciplinary difficulties. Many Nonconformist meetings were fairly small but, large or small, they mostly expected that all members would take an active part.

All the denominations, whether nationally or locally, published newspapers, magazines or just newsletters, many of which contain fascinating snippets about our ancestors. These can be time-consuming to browse and for the most part you have to give in to enjoying reading the old papers and not worry too much whether you find specific names. However, some newspapers have been indexed, or partly indexed as regards particular aspects; others may be digitized and suddenly become very easily searchable.

Nonconformists were often very active in local communities and may appear in the ordinary newspapers from time to time. Public campaigns or ceremonies or reports of church events may include large numbers of names. The national Nonconformist world was very good at mobilizing its members on issues of the day and you may find your ancestor's name on some petition. This adds nothing to the family tree, but a great deal to the family history.

Plymouth Brethren
In England the movement dates from a meeting held at Plymouth in 1831. Members were opposed to pretty well all forms of church government and believed in a strict life, keeping separate from the world and living a very plain life. The movement broke into segments as various people thought each other too lax in some regard. Some became known as Exclusive Brethren.

Mormons (Church of Jesus Christ of Latter Day Saints)
Mormonism first came to England in 1837 and was very successful, particularly among those who were not church attenders elsewhere (whatever their technical affiliation). The religious census of 1851 showed that 35,626 Mormons attended meetings on the census day. Conversions continued, but it was church policy to encourage converts to emigrate to Utah. There were just over 52,000 converts between 1851 and 1870, of whom just over 23,000 converted through Mormon channels. Taking into account any who emigrated on

their own and allowing for a level of lapsation in England, this naturally inhibited the build-up of a strong English base.

Mormons are well known for their commitment to tracing their ancestry and this goes back to the very early years of the movement.

See *Mormons in Early Victorian Britain*, Richard L. Jensen and Malcolm R. Thorp (eds) (University of Utah Press, 1989) and 'The Young and Tender Transplanted to Strengthen: Mormon emigrants from the British Isles', Ian Waller (*Genealogists' Magazine*, vol. 28, no. 12, December 2006).

The Salvation Army and other Christian missions

The problem of missionary work came to the fore at the end of the 18th century when England became responsible for governing large parts of India. Almost all English people were nominally Christian of some sort, but here was a country where almost everyone was 'heathen'. The days were gone (though not long gone) when Christians expected that to convert the rulers would mean that they simply instructed their subjects to convert.

Many Calvinists felt that attempting to convert people was interfering with the decisions

God had already made. The doctrine of the individual's inability to affect his own spiritual destiny obviously included his inability to help anyone else. Arminians, however, did not have that problem, and mission work to India was soon followed by mission work elsewhere. It was strengthened by the anti-slavery work to which English evangelicals were thoroughly committed. Once slaves were in charge of their own lives, it was high time to tell them that God loved them.

In England evangelicals were increasingly aware of a large body of people in the towns who did not attend church regularly. Even Anglicans were concerned at ignorance about Christian things and this all linked in to an increasing unhappiness with the ignorance of children – because there were no schools. Social and religious concerns went together.

The 19th century produced hundreds of societies intended to do religious, moral and social good. They had different emphases, but many of them have left extensive records. These are a wonderful source for *biography*, both the lives of those who worked for them and the lives of those they helped. They may be vital for family history in showing how and why people moved or that many people were born, married or died abroad, but as regards England the basic genealogical sources are going to be state registration (from 1837), the censuses (from 1841), wills, gravestones, etc. – the same as for everyone else.

The best known in England is the Salvation Army. In 1865 William Booth founded another Christian mission in the East End of London. It flourished and by 1878 there were 50 mission stations throughout England with 88 evangelists. In that year William's son Bramwell suggested the name Salvation Army. Almost immediately the image of an army took off and the mission formalized the use of uniform, ranks and a military language.

The Salvation Army developed a thorough record-keeping system for the adults who worked for it. It built many churches (called 'citadels') and there are records of the children dedicated there. Many citadels were licensed for marriage. Those who died were described as 'promoted to glory'.

The Salvation Army had no new theological position and was in the mainstream of 19th-century evangelical mission work. The fundamental genealogical records of its members will be found in the usual state sources. Its own records add colour to that; above all we are hoping for more information on the lives of individuals – the biography rather than the family history. See *My Ancestors were in the Salvation Army*, Ray Wiggins (Society of Genealogists, 1997).

Many other missionary societies have an archive and are well organized to tell people about their work and the people who worked for them. Almost all missionary societies produced newspapers, newsletters and publicity full of personal detail. Google the name of the organization you are interested in.

Catholic Apostolics (or Irvingites)
The Catholic Apostolic Church is best thought of as an early form of Pentecostal. Edward Irving was minister of a Scottish Church in London and began to emphasize the gifts of the spirit in a way which is now fairly mainstream, but was unheard-of in his day. The gifts of tongues and prophecy first appeared in his church in 1831, but other ministers were involved and Catholic Apostolics did not call themselves Irvingite. Members were received by laying-on of hands, but did not necessarily leave their former churches.

Catholic Apostolics had no connection with what we now call Catholics but were universally called Roman Catholics until the 20th century.

British Israelites
The British Israelites were a small group who believed that the British were the descendants of the Ten Lost Tribes of Israel. The titles of one of their popular pamphlets sums up the position: 'Forty Seven Identifications of the British Nation with the Lost House of Israel, founded upon 500 Scripture Proofs, showing the Tribe of Dan to have settled in North Ireland; the Welsh to be a tribe of Israel; the people of South Ireland to be the Canaanites, America to be identical with the Nation of Manasseh, Queen Victoria to be descended from David and our Coronation Stone in Westminster Abbey to be Jacob's Stone.'

This is in practice more of a genealogical theory than a religious one, but the idea that the English (possibly the British) are really the Chosen People mentioned in the Bible has a respectable history going back to the 1630s.

Others in the 19th century

There were many other smaller groups (including those who still ask when the bishops are going to open Joanna Southcott's box), but most of them had the general approach of other Nonconformists and were not very interested in the sacramental side of things or in keeping genealogical records. Their marriages and burials will be found in the same places as everyone else's and they were perfectly willing to comply with civil registration and the other systems of state record-keeping for which the Nonconformist body as a whole had pressed. Some were very much involved in the healing ministry and objected to worldly medical intervention. The Rev C.M. Davies (*Unorthodox London*, 1876) writes of the Plumstead Peculiars who were in trouble with the authorities for having allowed one of their children to die. He also visited the Walworth Jumpers – who presumably emphasized 'dancing before the Lord'.

Pentecostals, Seventh Day Adventists, Jehovah's Witnesses

These denominations were all important in the 20th century though the approach of Pentecostals has become very acceptable in some other churches and therefore they seem to be weakening as a separate denomination. The genealogy of their members is best researched through state records. Despite their specific theology all of them share a great deal of their approach with the Nonconformist traditions which are not interested in sacraments and formal church services. I am not aware of any categories of genealogical record that have no counterpart in the older groups.

The pure genealogy of families connected with the above groups – and others like them – starts with state sources. Their records of themselves are likely to be very interesting for individual biography, but not your first stop for building up the family tree. Many of their churches were independent, not centrally organized, and with no authority structure outside themselves. However, they mostly expected members to be very involved in the group and therefore their newsletters, newspapers and magazines are likely to mention a great many individuals of all ages. They also strongly valued and talked about the spiritual life and there are many accounts of people's conversions or wrestling with sin.

No. **192**

Date of Application ⟨‍⟩ Jul 25ᵏ 1906

Date of Marriage ⟨‍⟩ יום ל ל ׳ אב 566 6

Aug 13ᵏ 190 6

חתן ⟨‍⟩ הַ׳ ... ⟨‍⟩ אברהם ׳/

Morris Sanders

Address ... 57 Commercial St

Native of ... Leeds

Married before? No. Related to Bride?

Witness

Brothers (if any) יעקב ... צבי׳

Will attend Wedding No.

כלה ⟨‍⟩ ... אברבא

... מבי אוני.

Rebecca Lapin

Address ... 4 Ely Place. Whitechapel.

Native of ... Russia

Married before? No

Witness

Synagogue ... Old Montague St

Place of Celebration

Hour

Name of Celebrant

Chapter 4

Movement for the sake of religion

Ever since Paul and Barnabas sailed round the eastern Mediterranean establishing the early Churches, religion has always been a reason for moving about. However, in a book for family historians, I will limit myself to people we just might be able to trace a descent from!

The Middle Ages

Christianity's spiritual home was the Holy Land and its administrative headquarters was in Rome. Every year thousands of pilgrims went to Compostela in northwest Spain, and to Rome itself. In 1362 the English Hospice was founded there to give shelter to pilgrims and some sections of the visitors' book survive. Sometimes only numbers are given, but in 1446 there is a list of 46 pilgrims, mostly married couples, from the parish of Sutton Valence in Kent. In the early 1500s there is often some description of the pilgrim, for example

(January 1505) 'William Clifford, parish clerk of the Church of St Nicholas in Old Fish Street, London'; (March 1505) 'John Rawlin, a sailor, a native of Ludlow, wounded by robbers and half dead'; (14 June 1505) 'John Sheppard, captain of the ship St Anne'; and (5 April 1506) 'Maurice London, a sick Welshman, remained for sixteen days, and being unable to speak any other language, the Hospice was burthened with a Welsh interpreter to wait upon him.'

Opposition to pilgrimages was one of the main threads of the new thinking which led to Protestantism, and in the 1400s the Norfolk Lollards showed their disdain by referring to the British holy sites of Walsingham in Norfolk and Canterbury – where the famous shrine of St Thomas Becket drew pilgrims from far and wide – as 'Falsingham' and 'Cancerbury'. They said pilgrimages should be made 'to poor people' instead.

Pilgrimages did not completely stop at the Reformation, however. Protestants continued to go to Rome as part of the Grand Tour. The visitors' book of the English Hospice includes entries ranging from the great and the good, for example the poet John Milton, a guest in 1638, to ordinary people such as Thomas Stockton in 1585 'taken prisoner by the Turks and maimed' or in 1593 'Laurence Mellon, Irish, a soldier in the service of Sir William Stanley'.

The Reformation

The Reformation itself caused a great deal of movement and we are now more realistically in the period to which we can trace our ancestors.

The Dissolution of the Monasteries (1536–40) effectively made all the monks and nuns redundant. However, their names are all listed when they 'voluntarily' surrendered their houses and we then have lists of their pensions, which continued to be paid up to the 1570s. Those for the diocese of Lincoln (covering a number of counties) were published by the Lincoln Record Society in 1959. They give name, residence, pension, an indication of whether the pensioner was married and, eventually, date of death. A great deal of work has been done on the ex-religious of Yorkshire, and there is a project to compile a biographical index of all former monks and nuns. The original material for the whole country is in the National Archives. See 'The Dissolution of the Monasteries and Chantries: Sources in the National Archives', Aidan Lawes

(*Genealogists' Magazine*, vol. 27, no. 11, September 2003).

In the reign of Mary I (1553–8) many committed Protestants went abroad. Some spent time in Geneva, and Christina Garrett's *The Marian Exiles* gives biographical details of nearly 500 of them, including baptisms of children, burials of wives etc.

Most Protestant exiles came back to England early in the reign of Elizabeth I (1558–1603). So did many foreign Protestants from the Spanish Netherlands. From 1567 there was a huge influx to London, Canterbury, Colchester, Norwich and other towns in the southeast of England. They often came as family groups. Research into the background of those who came to Southampton shows that, of 51 people who came from Valenciennes, 26 were related to each other.

However, it is important to be clear about motives. Many immigrants did not come for reasons of religion but to work. By 1581 almost one-fifth (17 per cent) of the population of Norwich was from the Low Countries – and most of those were Protestant refugees. On the other hand a 'List of Strangers' in Dover in 1636 contains 46 Catholics and only 12 Protestants. Almost all of them were involved in sea trading, so perhaps none of them had come for reasons of religion.

There are a substantial number of surviving lists of 'strangers'. One for London in 1635 lists a couple of thousand foreign weavers. Most of them were Protestants, but they may not have come over because of religion. In Westminster, 23 out of 27 tailors in 1635 were French – probably Catholics working around the court of Queen Henrietta Maria, Charles I's queen. No doubt they left in 1642 when the Civil War began.

While people were coming in, others were going out. As persecution of Catholics increased in England some went to live abroad – there were English communities throughout the Spanish Netherlands. Some adults lived permanently in exile and there were increasing numbers of children, nuns and priests. By 1660 there were 40 institutions specifically for the English, many of which continued to function up to the French Revolution, when they transferred to England. A great many of their records have been published by the Catholic Record Society (CRS). Others have been published by the religious orders themselves.

Most Catholics abroad were gentry, but they naturally took their servants with them. It is not certain how many ordinary people went into permanent exile, but work on the records of those granted the freedom of some cities in the southern part of the Spanish Netherlands (approximately modern Belgium) has produced some very interesting results.

Not all Catholics went to Europe. In the 1630s Lord Baltimore attempted to establish Maryland in North America as a safe haven for Catholics, with limited success.

From the Civil War to the Jacobites

The English Civil War had political motives, but it was also a battle between Anglicans and Presbyterians. After the defeat of Charles I many royalists went abroad, and their exile was at least partly because of their religion. They returned after the Restoration but some of the children had to be naturalized, for example, in 1661, Charlotte Boyle 'born at Paris in France, daughter to Francis, Viscount Shannon, brother to the Earl of Corke'.

Catholics and High Church Anglicans were not the only groups to go abroad. As early as the reign of Elizabeth I, John Smith, who is often regarded as the founder of the Baptist movement, went to Amsterdam. The registers of his congregation there between 1598 and

1617 show people from Southampton, Hurst Castle, Salisbury, Newbury, Warminster, Frome, Selwood, Westbury, Beckington, Hilperton, Bradford-on-Avon, Chippenham, Wrington, Wells, Bruton, Taunton and Weymouth. However, some English people did not want to live with foreigners even if their religion was right. The Pilgrim Fathers on the *Mayflower* established New England and were followed by perhaps 20,000 other emigrants between 1620 and 1640. It is impossible to assess how many went chiefly for reasons of religion and how many went just for land, but such emigrants must have been at least sympathetic to the Puritan way of worship.

Later in the century Quakers also emigrated. William Penn was given a grant of land ('Pennsylvania') in 1681, and about 1,000 Quakers a year emigrated between 1681 and 1686. By 1700 there were about 13,000 Quakers in the North American colonies. The earlier Puritans had stemmed largely from the eastern counties of England. Quakers were largely from the north, above all Cheshire.

While Quakers were leaving the North of England, French Protestant Huguenots were coming into the South. Around the time of the Revocation of the Edict of Nantes in 1685 it is estimated that about 60,000 French people came to Great Britain (40,000 went to London and 20,000 elsewhere, including Ireland). They established their own Church and kept very good records, many of which have been published by the Huguenot Society of Great Britain and Ireland. These often give clear evidence as to where the family had come from in France. Some went on, particularly to New York, Virginia and South Carolina.

There were some congregations in the West of England but none in the North, although individual craftsmen may have settled anywhere. The short-lived congregations at Thorney, Cambridgeshire, and Sandtoft, Lincolnshire, are sometimes referred to as Huguenots, but their members had come over to England to help in draining the fens and religion was not the reason for their move.

In fact, in 1685 Huguenots were coming to a country with a Catholic king. For three years (1685–8) England was uneasy under James II, and much of the population was glad to see the back of him. Some loyalists followed him abroad. Jacobites were not really religious exiles, but their loyalty was often a consequence of their High Anglican or Catholic beliefs. For the next 50 years there were communities of Jacobites abroad. After the failed rebellions of 1715 and 1745–6 many ordinary people were transported to America as a punishment for taking part. The treason for which they were punished was a consequence of their sympathy for the religion of the Stuarts.

Ireland had also had its fair share of religious troubles: the Plantation of Scots Protestants to Ulster; the removal of the Gaelic Irish 'To Hell or Connaught'; and the Flight of the 'Wild Geese' into Europe, which transplanted Catholic Irish to every Catholic country in the world, with the result that the liberator of Chile was Bernardo O'Higgins and one President of France was a MacMahon. Protestant Irish also left Ulster in large numbers because of the economic laws against any trade which would compete with England. This was not religious persecution as such, but it reflected the general policy of keeping the Irish down.

When Southern Ireland was establishing its independence religious pressure was the other way. Between 1911 and 1926 the Church of Ireland population fell by 34 per cent – from 250,00 to 164,000. The 17th-century troubles in Scotland between Covenanters and Episcopalians were equally severe, but did not give rise to any great migrations.

After 1750

While religious enthusiasm waned in England, Americans were beginning to come back. John Woolman, the Quaker, came to England in 1772 to preach against the slave trade, and in 1807 Lorenzo Dow brought to England the tradition of 'camp meetings', revivalist born-again Pentecostal-style Christian worship, which began at Mow Cop in Staffordshire. The tradition has carried on ever since.

Missionaries were also beginning to go out from the United Kingdom, first to Asia and then to Africa. These were not mass movements, but the social consequences were enormous. The numbers were in fact very substantial when we remember the tens of thousands of priests and nuns who went out from Ireland. From the 1860s the Irish almost single-handedly took on Christian conversion of the English-speaking world and priests and nuns worked throughout Africa, Asia and the British Empire. No history of Australia, Canada or America is complete which ignores the contribution of Irish Catholicism to their growth. Life as a missionary was never easy; many lost their lives. About 60 Protestant missionaries were killed in the Boxer Rising in China in 1900.

The period 1830–1930 saw massive emigra-

Revocation or Revolution?

Many people speculate that their ancestors were French and often wonder if they may have come over at the time of the French Revolution. This refers primarily to the 1790s when many aristocrats and Catholic clergy and their servants came to England to escape persecution. The vast majority of the Catholic clergy eventually returned to France, but some of the other French exiles may have remained and founded families.

However, people often mix up the French Revolution with the Revocation of the Edict of Nantes in 1685. This was the point at which Protestantism became illegal in France and, sooner or later, many French Protestants came to England. Revolution? Revocation? A hundred years apart and not connected.

Many French people have come to England over the centuries for reasons which had nothing to do with religion.

tion from Europe to the rest of the world, including child migration from Britain to Canada, Australia and New Zealand. The practice needs to be seen in the context of its time. One reason why *Catholic* children were sent to Canada was the sense that they would be safer, spiritually, in Catholic Quebec than in Protestant England. The records of the receiving orphanage in Rimouski in Canada give details of origin which the records of the sending organizations over here do not.

There were other gains and losses. The French Revolution had begun by being very anti-Christian, and many thousands of priests fled. Throughout the 1790s there were about 5,000 French Catholic priests in England – all on state pensions – with an incredible 500 living in Winchester at one time. Almost all of them went home after peace was signed (for the first time) in 1802. Later in the century many European liberals took refuge in England against reactionary or conservative states – in many cases this was because they were against religion, either altogether or in its 19th-century form.

The last great 19th-century movement was that of the Jews. After 1881 they became the objects of substantial persecution in the Russian Empire, and over the next 25 years about a million emigrated. Most of them intended to go to America, but many ended up in England. They arrived as victims of a persecution which was basically religious, since Jews who converted to Christianity were no longer subject to legal penalties.

Not all population movement was the result of persecution. At the best of times the clergy were always a mobile class, moving from one parish to another as they rose up the career ladder. During the Civil War many Anglican clergy lost their livings, and after the Restoration many of the Puritan clergy were forced out by the Act of 1662 – which forbade them to go within five miles of their previous parishes. Many committed Christians saw root-lessness as a virtue, and up until our own day it has been standard practice for Methodist ministers to move every three years.

See *Letters of Denization and Acts of Naturalization 1603–1700*, W.A. Shaw (Huguenot Society, vol. 18, 1911); Catholic Record Society publications *passim*; Huguenot Society publications *passim*.

Chapter 5

Catholic and Jacobite records

From 1559 to 1778 Roman Catholic services were illegal in England and Wales and the laws against Catholics were very severe. They were not always operated, but it was always necessary for Catholics to keep their heads down. Apart from religious prejudice there was a strong feeling that Catholics could not be trusted as they had two loyalties – to the Pope as well as the monarch.

The establishment of the Church of England in 1533–4 did not mean that England became a Protestant country immediately. Henry VIII was concerned with divorce, and with selling the property of the church to make money. The Dissolution of the Monasteries (1536–40) was initially founded on accusations that the monks and nuns were not carrying out their religious duties properly, not that those duties were wrong. The monks and nuns were eventually sent away but all received pensions –

redundancy money, as we would say – and were not released from their vows of celibacy during his reign.

Under Edward VI (1547–53) England moved in a Protestant direction and under Mary I (1553–8) the pendulum swung back. Elizabeth I established a form of Anglicanism which was concerned with outward obedience; there was no persecution of people who would attend quietly and say nothing. Most Anglican ministers had been Catholic priests under the former regime and had a great deal of freedom in their own parish churches. This policy worked; both Puritans and Catholics basically stayed inside the national church.

The situation changed dramatically for Catholics in the late 1570s and early 1580s. New priests, trained in the seminaries of the Counter-Reformation, began to convert English people back to Catholicism while the Dutch Revolt, which Elizabeth had supported tacitly for years, flared into full-scale war between England and Spain.

In 1581 and 1585 the laws about church attendance were strengthened and enforced. Those who refused to attend church were known as recusants (from a Latin word meaning 'they refuse'). Influential Catholics were imprisoned, losing their lands and even their lives if their religion led them to commit treason. Many priests were hung, drawn and quartered, and the life expectancy of one in England was close to that of a 2nd Lieutenant in the First World War trenches.

The Gunpowder Plot of 1605 sealed the fate of all Catholics in the Protestant mind – they must be traitors. By this time Catholicism had been rooted out of many counties in England. Working-class Catholicism hardly survived at all, but upper-class Catholics (able and willing to bear the brunt of the heavy fines) could stand their ground. A great many lived in the North of England. In Yorkshire in 1604 it was estimated that only four per cent of the population was Catholic – but 25 per cent of gentry.

Where the gentry were able to provide protection, yeomen and tradesmen could continue as Catholics. Thus the pattern was set for the next 200 years – specific parishes, particularly in the North, where the chief family was Catholic and sheltered a priest, surrounded by dozens of other parishes with no Catholics at all, or numbers in single figures.

Lancashire was far and away the most Catholic county in England. Perhaps a third of the population of the areas called the Fylde and Amounderness was Catholic throughout the 17th and 18th centuries. Next came Northumberland, Durham and the North Riding of Yorkshire with between five and eight per cent, then Staffordshire and Worcestershire. Some southern counties had a dozen or so centres, but others, such as Bedfordshire, Buckinghamshire and Cambridgeshire, had only one each and Huntingdonshire had none.

London was always a special case. Foreigners were not subject to the law in religion and the embassies of Catholic countries kept a large staff to minister to English (and Irish) Catholics as well as their own.

Moreover, the Court was in London. All the Stuart kings had Catholic wives and mothers whose marriage settlements permitted them freedom of worship, so that there were legal Catholic services every day in the royal palaces. Puritans were appalled. These services obviously stopped during the Civil War and Commonwealth, but were revived when Charles II came to the throne.

In fact, except at times of special crisis, the pressure on Catholics had lifted. Low Church and High Church Anglicans were too busy contending with each other. After 1662 the courts were full of 'sectaries' being presented for non-attendance at church, and it is often impossible to distinguish them from 'papists'.

The Glorious Revolution gave Nonconformists freedom of worship (with various political disabilities), but Catholicism remained illegal. Catholics were now supposed to be automatic Jacobites, but most, despite a sentimental preference for a Catholic monarch, knew that he had not a chance of winning the throne.

This is a point which must be repeated. Jacobites were people who supported James II and his son and grandson – the Old Pretender and the Young Pretender, all of whom were Catholics. Many High Anglicans believed that replacing James with William of Orange was wrong, and that the later Hanoverian kings had no right to the throne. This was not basically a religious question, since many Anglican Jacobites did not like the fact that the 'rightful' king was a Catholic.

Toleration and legality came suddenly from an unexpected quarter. With the conquest of Canada in 1759, England was responsible for a Catholic nation which it wished to make loyal. Accepting Canadian Catholicism made the illegality of English Catholicism seem an anomaly, and the War Office pressed the point. When the American Revolutionary War broke out,

Catholic emancipation

Many people think that the Catholic Emancipation Act of 1829 was the point at which Catholicism became legal (whether in England or Ireland) and that persecution had continued – and been severe – up to that point. This is not so. Catholic services were made legal in England and Wales in 1778 and the building of Catholic churches was permitted in 1791. In Ireland, mass was widely and openly available from the early 1700s.

However, Catholics (like Nonconformists) were unable to rise socially because many middle- and upper-class activities required an Anglican communion certificate or an Oath of Loyalty to the monarch as head of the Anglican Church – and Catholics and Nonconformists were mostly unwilling to take Anglican communion or swear such an oath. The Act of 1829 was not about the practice of Catholicism, but about releasing middle-class Catholics (primarily) from the social and career disabilities which being a Catholic brought them.

large numbers of recruits to the army were needed from Ireland and the Highlands of Scotland (which had substantial pockets of Catholicism). Religious services – Catholic services – were required and these had to be legal. The Emancipation Act of 1778 was pushed through in a few months.

In the 1840s, Catholic numbers and influence exploded. Tens of thousands of poor Irish flooded into the northern industrial towns as a result of the Potato Famine in Ireland. They dramatically increased the visibility of Catholics in the North. At the same time, numbers of High Anglicans began to convert. They were prosperous, influential and confident that many more of their sort would follow them. Thirdly, many ordinary English people, especially in the Midlands, were converted by three charismatic Italian missionaries – Rosmini, Barberi and Gentili. From then on Catholics were very visible in the mainstream.

The records

These divide into three categories: state records; Anglican records; and the Catholics' records of themselves. Much useful material is published by the Catholic Record Society (CRS) and most family historians should start by browsing their volumes. There are also good Catholic local history societies for some areas (the North, the North West, the South West, Staffordshire and Worcestershire (later combining as the Midlands), Kent and Gloucester). Two journals, *London Recusant* and *Essex Recusant*, published excellent articles, but are now defunct.

Two bibliographies (one for general and one

for local sources) analyse these and a great deal of other material in *Catholic family history: a bibliography of general sources* (M. Gandy, 1996), arranged by category, and *Catholic family history: a bibliography of local sources* (M. Gandy, 1996), arranged by county.

State records

The main sources are:

Quarter Sessions

From 1559–1642 the only source for most ordinary Catholics is their presentation at Quarter Sessions for non-attendance at church. Unless they were very active, they were not likely to be more than fined.

Presentment was not systematic. It depended on the efficiency or commitment of the local minister or churchwardens, and the extent to which they were under pressure from central government or swayed by political events such as the Armada or the Gunpowder Plot. There must have been many Catholics who were not presented, or not so often as they could have been.

During the Civil War and Commonwealth there was no national church, so neither Catholics nor anyone else were presented for not attending it. After 1662 Catholics were presented in great numbers, but the real heat was on Protestant Nonconformists and the records do not always say why particular individuals were presented – Catholics, Baptists and Quakers may be listed together.

Although Catholicism remained illegal after 1689, neither magistrates nor churchwardens were proactive in presenting Catholics. However, there was a substantial reward for informers, so prominent Catholics and priests were presented from time to time. The last priest to be sentenced to life imprisonment was John Baptist Moloney in 1767, who served three years.

Assize records
These contain information on Catholics in serious trouble, such as priests and those who sheltered them.

Pipe Rolls and Recusant Rolls
For the better-off people, fines were very damaging. Once they were officially 'convicted' then there were a number of legal disabilities and land could be confiscated. Convictions were recorded in the Exchequer Pipe Rolls in 1581–92 (all listed in CRS 71) and are now in

the National Archives (E 372). From 1592 to 1691 there are separate Recusant Rolls (E 376 and 377), but unfortunately only the first four (1592–6) have been published (CRS 18, 57, 61). These are annual (except for the Commonwealth period) and arranged by county. A good deal of information is given about the convicted recusant's land, but there is no genealogical background.

The Lord Treasurer's Remembrancer's Memoranda Rolls

Convicted recusants could go through a process of conformity, eventually involving taking holy communion in an Anglican church and presenting evidence of this. Numbers of upper-class Catholics did this and a list of the names for 1590–1625 (arranged by county) was published in *Catholic Ancestor* (the journal of the Catholic Family History Society) between June 1995 and November 1996. See also 'Sources for Conformity in Elizabethan and Jacobean England' by Michael Questier (*Catholic Ancestor*, vol. 5, no. 5, June 1995). The aim (leaving religious motives aside) was to recover sequestrated lands and get discharged from their recusancy fines. Since money comes into it, the records were returned to central government, and are now at the National Archives in E 368.

Civil War records
Catholics suffered with other royalists after the king's defeat. Records such as those of the Commission for Compounding with Delinquents mention when a royalist was also a recusant.

Returns of papists
During the 1580s government was concerned to have lists of Catholics who might be traitors, but they were really only concerned with people of importance. At other times (such as the Compton census of 1676) they were concerned with numbers, not names. In the 18th century Catholics were listed three times: 1705, 1767 and 1780. Some of the returns (in the House of Lords Record Office) are only statistical; others have names. Many of the fair copies sent up to London were taken from longer lists – with names – retained by Quarter Sessions. The 1767 Return has been published by the CRS and is particularly good for South Lancashire (which had more Catholics than anywhere else). A copy of the London Return of 1767 (taken from an original at

Lambeth Palace) is in the Society of Genealogists' library.

Registration of papists' and nonjurors' estates
After the Jacobite Rebellion of 1715 all Catholics refusing the Oaths of Loyalty and Supremacy had to register their names and property at Quarter Session. A full list of the owners' names is at the National Archives in the series list in E 174, but the returns often include the names of tenants and occupiers, who may not be Catholics.

State Papers Domestic
There are references to Catholics at all levels of society. The printed calendars for the 16th and 17th centuries index references, but the indexes are to the calendars rather than the documents; imaginative browsing can be very productive. They are particularly valuable for prominent Catholics: courtiers, recalcitrant gentlewomen and, of course, priests.

The formal records of priests and prisoners have been thoroughly worked over by Catholic historians. Many of the best sources were written by the representatives of Catholic countries and sent home, or by Catholics in exile. Despite the vast amount of work done on martyrs, the family background of many of them is still uncertain.

Privy Council and Treasury papers
These have unsystematic references to individuals, for example permission for certain Catholics to travel more than five miles from home.

Anglican records

The law was concerned with outward behaviour, not inner belief. Non-Anglicanism was a legal crime, not a form of heresy or moral turpitude, and Catholics were not tried for their behaviour or beliefs in the ecclesiastical courts. The records of convicted recusants who chose to conform are discussed above (see E 368). Catholics were hardly ever excommunicated (but see C 207 just in case).

In practice many Catholics were married and buried in the Church of England – the problem is usually with baptisms, and not always then. Catholics used the usual systems for marriage licences and proving wills. Both the Church and local government were controlled by the local gentry with the result that, since Catholicism was mostly an upper-class religion, Catholic gentry were appointing Church of England ministers and sitting on the magistrates' bench hearing presentments.

For a short period from 1696 Anglican ministers were supposed to record non-Anglican events as well. In practice this habit died away by about 1704, but in some Lancashire parishes Catholic baptisms and marriages were recorded, and explicitly described as such, for many years after. See various registers of South Lancashire published by the Lancashire Parish Register Society.

Catholic records

Catholic priests knew the importance of recording baptisms, confirmations and marriages, but until the 18th century few of them dared to do it – or, at least, only a tiny handful of notebooks have survived. Many registers begin in the mid-18th century.

Entries of baptism usually give the names of the parents (including the mother's maiden name), the date of birth as well as baptism, and the names of the godparents. Entries of confirmation are rare for this early date as there was no proper system of bishops, but during the reign of James II Bishop Leyburn was appointed. In 1687 he travelled round the North of England and confirmed about 20,000 people. The names have been published by the North West Catholic History Society. Presumably he intended to do Southern England as soon as possible, but his plans were overtaken by the king's abdication.

Entries of marriage may be minimalist. After Lord Hardwicke's Marriage Act of 1753 Catholics were all married in the Church of England, but there may have been a second ceremony as well and records of some of these survive. Deaths and notes of anniversaries are fairly frequent but not systematic, since neither death nor burial is a sacrament.

Thus for ordinary Catholics there may be no specifically Catholic records before about 1750. However, Catholics appear in all the standard non-religious sources. Records, which are extensive, mostly relate to the clergy, their families and the actions of those who helped them.

In 1568 Cardinal Allen established a seminary at Douai to train priests for the English mission. Over the next 50 years a number of other colleges opened, some for secular priests (those responsible to a bishop in a diocese) and others for the main religious orders: Benedictines, Carmelites, Dominicans, Franciscans, Jesuits. Many Englishwomen had also gone abroad to be nuns and from the 1590s there was an increasing number of specifically English convents abroad, mostly in the Spanish Netherlands and Northern France. All these organizations soon began to educate boys and girls and for nearly 200 years these were used by generations of the same families. Many colleges and convent schools came back to England in the 1790s and still survive as the major Catholic public schools, such as Ampleforth, Downside and Stonyhurst.

The records of all these institutions (at their height there were about 40 of them) are extensive. Many are published by the CRS; others have been published independently.

The majority of nuns in this period lived enclosed, domestic lives of prayer, but the convent necrologies sum up their lives at death and give us a picture of their characters. The lives of the men, especially before the Civil War, were much more dangerous since they were sent to England. The records of their training (abroad) are very good (many have been published by the CRS) and their deaths are usually documented – but we cannot always know what they did in the years when they travelled around England hiding identities under false names. Those who were caught and imprisoned, tortured or martyred are usually well-documented as regards their end but, even for them, much is unknown.

Most poor Catholics appear in the Anglican records and Catholics are in all the mainstream genealogical records of the 19th century. (It is sometimes said that Irish Catholics would not have co-operated with the British government's system of registration, but there is no evidence of this at all.) Many ordinary families in the North of England have a tradition of having been continuously Catholic since before the Reformation. Despite the difficulty of tracing back through the 17th century, this seems very likely to be true, particularly for families with roots in parts of Lancashire and the North Riding of Yorkshire.

See *Tracing Catholic Ancestry*, Michael Gandy (Federation of Family History Societies, 1998) and 'Sources for Recusants in English Official Archives', J.A. Williams, *Recusant History*, vol. 16, no. 4 (Catholic Record Society, 1983).

Chapter 6

Huguenot records

In the 16th and 17th centuries about 10 per cent of the population of France was Protestant, following the beliefs and style of worship developed by John Calvin. They were called Huguenots. The nearest equivalent in England and Scotland were the Presbyterians.

After a long civil war the Edict of Nantes in 1598 guaranteed Protestants freedom of worship. From the 1660s, however, they came under increasing pressure from Louis XIV and the Catholic majority. Their numbers went down and in 1685 Protestantism was made illegal by the Revocation of the Edict of Nantes. The remaining Protestants became Catholics outwardly, their 'temples' were closed and their baptisms, marriages and burials appear in the Catholic parish registers.

The Huguenots in Britain

Even before the Revocation some Huguenots had decided to emigrate to Protestant countries such as Holland and the Calvinist parts of Switzerland. The English were also very welcoming, and between 1685 and the early 18th century an estimated 60,000 Huguenots came to England, mostly to London and towns in the southeast of England. There were some settlements in the West Country, primarily in Bristol and Plymouth. None existed in the Midlands or the North of England or Wales and, perhaps more surprisingly, there were none in Scotland. However, an unknown (fairly large) number went to Ireland where the government was trying to encourage Protestant settlement. These included weavers, who went to help establish the linen trade in Ulster, and many retired French army officers. When peace broke out they went onto half pay (and might live anywhere), but the condition of receiving a pension was settling in Ireland.

Huguenots came from all social classes. In London (where about 40,000 went) the poorer Huguenots settled mostly in Spitalfields and Bethnal Green, both still part of the large parish of Stepney. Wealthier Huguenots settled in Westminster, particularly in the parish of St Anne, Soho. Other more suburban Huguenot communities included Islington, Wandsworth,

Greenwich and even Sunbury-on-Thames.

Huguenots were not found equally all over France, but clustered in four areas: Northeastern France (near the modern Belgian border); Normandy; Western France near to La Rochelle (the provinces of Aunis, Saintonge and Poitou); and Languedoc in Southwest France. Unsurprisingly, many of the immigrants to England were from Normandy and Northeastern France.

When the Huguenots began to arrive there were two French churches in London: Threadneedle Street in the City and the Savoy Church in Westminster. By 1700 there were 24, but as the older generation of French speakers died out the congregations began to dwindle. By 1800 all the London churches had closed and there is now just one French Protestant church – in Soho. The children and grandchildren of the original immigrants intermarried with their English neighbours and began to go to the local Anglican or other Nonconformist churches.

There are also French Protestant churches in Canterbury and Southampton, but they themselves do not have any early genealogical records. Their early material has been published by the Huguenot Society.

The heart of the community was the silk-weaving area of London's East End. When the home-based weaving trade was destroyed by mechanization in the mid-19th century, many Huguenot descendants moved up to the hosiery towns of the East Midlands. However, the immigrants did not go there straight from France and there are no special records.

The Huguenots' own records

The Huguenot churches kept records of baptisms and marriages. All the known registers were handed into public keeping with the other Nonconformist records and are now in the National Archives in RG 4. These contain registers of the Walloon and French Protestant churches in England and the French Chapel Royal at St James's Palace. They have all been in print for many years, published by the Huguenot Society, whose library and archives are held at University College, London. Most have recently been republished on CD-ROM. Simplified forms of the entries appear on the Mormon IGI/FamilySearch.

None of the Huguenot chapels had burying grounds; their burials were in the Church of England churchyards. For the East End communities, names will be found above all in the registers of St Dunstan, Stepney. Over the years new churches were built in that area: the registers of Christ Church, Spitalfields, begin in 1729 and those of St Matthew, Bethnal Green, in 1746. In the West End the registers of St Anne, Soho, begin in 1685. Other Huguenots were buried in the Nonconformist burying ground of Bunhill Fields, but unfortunately the earliest registers of that are lost. The surviving registers begin in 1713.

Baptisms nearly always give the birth date of the child as well as the baptism date. They also mostly give the maiden name of the mother. They also give the names of the god-parents, who were often relatives. The French language has a lot of letters that are silent, so the problem of spelling variations is even worse than in English. The name Heraud, for example, could be Heraut, Herault, Eraud, Eyraud, Ayrault, Heros – to name but a few!

Marriages often give the names of the parents – both father and mother, including the mother's maiden name. They also give residence or place of birth and this can be a vital clue to the place of origin in France. Huguenots, like Scottish Presbyterians, some-times recorded the date the couple gave in their names for proclamation rather than the actual date of marriage, some weeks later.

The French chapels had a system of membership. New arrivals presented a character reference (*témoignage*) from their previous church to demonstrate they were in good standing. A large number survive, particularly for the great church of Threadneedle Street. They often show that the new members had not come direct from France but were moving from Holland, particularly from Amsterdam, Haarlem and Utrecht, or from Canterbury, or from other churches in London.

One helpful aspect is that young people who had grown up in the church often presented a reference when they were old enough to become independent members. Thus there are a lot of references to teenagers, often sponsored by their parents or guardians (who are named) and stated to be born in London.

Other arrivals did not have a character reference. Those who had converted outwardly in France in 1685 (after the Revocation of the Edict of Nantes) had to 'confess their fault' to the elders and deacons in the consistory. Names are recorded, often with large groups of other people just arrived from the same place.

The records of the consistory show the church authorities dealing with problems of

Did you know?

It often comes as a surprise to English people to learn that when Louis XIV declared Protestantism illegal, in 1685, all French Protestants converted to Catholicism within the next few months. This was outward conformity – but that was what was required – and they did it because they had a very high view of the authority of the king.

For family historians this has a double benefit. An almost total census of French Protestants in 1685 can be derived from Catholic registers in which their 'abjurations from heresy' were recorded. Later, when they arrived in the various Protestant countries to which they fled, they presented themselves before the consistory and confessed their fault and did penance. Thus we can date their flight fairly exactly and, as a bonus, often get a statement of where they had come from.

behaviour, such as disputes between family members or masters and servants. Not all the information is negative – one deaf old lady was given permission to sit right under the pulpit. These have been translated and published for the vital years of 1679–92. For many years before and afterwards they are on microfilm. Unpublished material is mostly in French.

The French chapels all had a well-developed system for supporting their own poor. Elders all had their own area (known as a *quartier*) and collected the poor contributions from better-off members of the church. There are then extensive records of how the money was distributed: regular payments to those in long-term need and casual payments to others.

There were also specific charities. The French Hospital was founded in 1718 to be a home for elderly or incapable Huguenots. As the years went by and the old immigrants died off, it required evidence of descent from an immigrant ancestor. The 19th-century applications thus contain a great deal of genealogical proof sent in by ordinary Cockneys with a French great-grandfather. There were charity schools for boys and girls, and the churches also administered bequests which helped pay for apprenticeships to set young people up in business. The Coqueau Charity was one of these and people used to remember their grandmother being 'on the cocoa'.

Some of the early Huguenots formed societies for dinner and gossip. Over the years these societies also began to help their poorer members. There are records of the Society of the Parisians, the Society of Saintonge, the Society of Normans (and the more specific Society of Lintot, which is in Normandy). Nearly all these records are held at the

Huguenot Society near Euston station in London. Some have been published and many others are available on microfilm.

Huguenots appear in all the general records for tracing anyone in England, but there are a few more specific ones. Many chose to be naturalized (or endenizened, a simpler formality which permitted them to trade). These records are in the National Archives in HO 1; those to 1800 have been published by the Huguenot Society. Copies of sacrament certificates of those naturalized under the statute are in E 196/10, and are published by the Huguenot Society, vol. XXXV (1932), pp. 11–33.

When the first rush of refugees arrived in the 1680s, there were collections for them all over England. The money was administered through the King's (or Queen's) Bounty. Some hundreds of notebooks of the payments made were all computerized some years ago, and you may find many entries to small payments made to the same people. These usually give a statement of residence, which may be an address in London or their place of origin in France.

A great many poor Huguenots in the East End were weavers, and the records of the Weavers' Company give a lot of information on the existence of 'foreign masters' and the apprenticeships of young people. These can help to date when a family first arrived. Most of the immigrants came in the 1680s and 1690s, but a steady stream (declining to a trickle) continued to emigrate from France right up to the 1760s. By that time it would be hard to know if their motives were primarily religious or economic, but if they got involved with the French Protestant churches in England then presumably they had a Protestant background in France.

One word of warning. A French name does not have to mean the family were from France. Many 'Huguenots' in ordinary records came from the Channel Islands – not part of France and wholly Protestant from the 1540s.

Also, a reminder that Protestant Huguenots were not the only French people to come to England. French ancestors may have come over because of the Norman Conquest, the wine trade with Bordeaux, the French Revolution, even the First World War. The popularity of French fashion and cooking has always meant a steady stream of dressmakers, milliners, chefs, ladies' maids, governesses and language teachers. The vast majority of these would have been Catholics.

Tracing Huguenot ancestry in France

With the help of records in England it is very often possible to find out where in France a family had come from. French Catholic parish registers often go back to the early 17th century, or even the 16th century, and there are other sources similar to those we have in England. One advantage is the custom of noting contracts publicly, so there are many records of marriage contracts and land transfers between members of very ordinary families. These records are not about religion.

The survival of Huguenot church registers is very patchy. For many hundreds of 'temples' closed before 1685 nothing survives at all, and we are dependent on annual copies (equivalent to Bishops' Transcripts though submitted to the state authorities). These date from 1667. In other cases there are good registers of baptisms, marriages and burials going back to the 1560s. All the known registers are listed, with other material, in *Les Familles Protestantes en France* by Gildas Bernard, published by the Archives Nationales in Paris in 1987. The *Société de l'Histoire du Protestantisme Français* in Paris has an excellent series of register transcripts, as well as copies of many local histories of Protestants in particular areas.

Chapter 7

Jewish records

Jews came into Northern Europe by one of two routes. Sephardic (Spanish) Jews are those who came via north Africa into Spain, from which most of them were expelled in the 1490s. They are likely to have come to England from Holland. Jews in Portugal shared the cultural characteristics of Spanish Jews. These are generalizations.

Ashkenazi (German) Jews came north from Italy and settled in various states within modern Germany and Austria. Many may eventually have come to England direct from there, but in the 17th century many migrated eastwards, leading to a 200-year history in Russia and Poland. The situation is complicated as Poland was not a separate state between 1795 and 1918. Other Jews, for example from Romania, lived under the Turkish Empire before it began to contract.

The medieval Jewish community in England was expelled in 1290. From Elizabethan times there was a small community of Portuguese Jews who kept their religion secret. It is unlikely that there were many outside London, and in most parts of England we may say firmly that there were none.

Jewish settlement in Britain

In 1656 a group of Sephardic Jews from Holland petitioned for permission to open a synagogue in London. They were mostly merchants with connections in both countries and it is not likely that they thought of themselves as immigrants. By 1690 there were enough German Jews to found a synagogue of their own. During the 18th century the two communities were fairly equal in numbers, but the balance shifted steadily in favour of Jews of the German tradition. By the late 19th century they were probably ten times more in number than Jews of the Spanish tradition. They were still largely in London and most of the communities elsewhere were pretty small.

By 1880 there were about 47,000 Jews in London, fairly balanced across the classes. According to the Post Office Directory of 1848, 25 per cent of Jewish traders were in Bloomsbury. By 1861 there were about 1,000 Jews in Canonbury and Barnsbury and by 1880

Numbers and names

Jewish records are dated according to the Jewish calendar (see *Dates and Calendars for the Genealogist*, Cliff Webb, Society of Genealogists, for a simple explanation). When dates have been transposed to the Christian calendar, remember that our ancestors – like us – could get their arithmetic wrong.

Jews often combined surnames with a patronymic system. They were also prepared to simplify, alter or translate names to make easier. Immigrants from Eastern Europe had to decide on a spelling in the English (Latin) alphabet instead of either the Hebrew or the Cyrillic (Russian) alphabet. Thus the same name may have very different spellings which more or less represent the same sound.

about 2,000 Jews in Maida Vale. The community was about to be utterly changed.

The assassination of Tsar Alexander II of Russia in 1881 led to persecution, and many Jews left Russia to escape that. However, the Cossack pogroms which are so well known (if only from *Fiddler on the Roof*) did not take place all over Russia. Many Jews left for economic reasons which were not basically different from the reasons prompting country people all over Europe to leave the country for a life in the industrial towns, whether in Europe or America. There were, for example, no Cossacks in Lithuania.

For many Jews from Eastern Europe, England was a staging post on the way to America. They got off at Hull, travelled across England by train and re-shipped at Liverpool. Many others, however, chose to stay in England where there were no formalities about settlement until 1905.

By 1914 there were about 150,000 Jews in London. The largest community was in the East End of London, but there were about 10,000 Jews in West London, 20,000 in North and Northeast London, 6,000–7,000 in Northwest London and 5,000–6,000 in South London. The second largest community was in Leeds, and there were other big communities in Manchester, Liverpool, the Northeast and Glasgow. Whether they came from town or country before their migration, within the British Isles they almost all settled in towns.

However, we must not think of Jews as a group who were all the same. Dutch merchants and German middle-class Jews had little in common with poor country Jews from the East, and were divided rather than unified by the different styles and traditions that their religion had developed locally. By the end of the 19th century many Jewish families had been in Britain for generations and were pretty anglicized. Those still practising their religion shaded into those who followed Jewish cultural practices without being assiduous in synagogue attendance to those who had married out, or converted, or simply had no connection with the community.

The Jewish religion in Britain

This book is concerned with religion, not race or nationality, and the focus here is not upon Jews as foreigners or on Jewish social customs. As a religion, Judaism was completely legal in this country from 1657 and under Lord Hardwicke's Marriage Act Jews were exempted from the rule that everyone must marry in the Anglican Church. Likewise Jews were permitted their own burying grounds and the cemetery at Mile End opened in 1657. Jews, like Nonconformists and Catholics, were excluded from those areas of public life for which an Anglican communion certificate was required, but these exclusions did not affect poor people. Those laws were repealed in the 19th century.

Moreover, Christians found Judaism, as a religion, psychologically acceptable (not for themselves but for Jews). Bible readers could find Jewish practices ordained by God in the

Old Testament and many Nonconformists found themselves conscientiously bound to follow various instructions which God gave the Jews. Thus (and this is not a quibble) to many Anglicans and Nonconformists Judaism was right in its day but superseded, whereas Catholicism (to take the extreme case) was a perversion of Christianity as they saw it.

Some Christians saw Jews as a particularly important field for missionary work. They felt that God had not really abandoned the Jews as the Chosen People and that therefore it was particularly pleasing to him that Jews should accept Jesus. Some took this further and felt that the Second Coming would not occur until all the Jews had been converted, so evangelism among them was particularly important as a means of bringing that about. There are thus a number of Christian Missions to the Jews which may give both general cultural and specific anecdotal information about Jews.

Early records of Jews

The early religious records of Jews (say, to 1837) are not extensive, but have been thoroughly worked on by Jewish researchers. The genealogical material is available either in published form or through the Mormons. The marriage records are fairly informative and are supplemented by copies of marriage contracts which may have been (but were not necessarily) deposited with the synagogue. There are also extensive burial records.

The chief problem is with records of birth. Circumcision (universal for Jewish boys) was not a synagogue ceremony and the synagogues have no records of them. Specialist surgeons (*mohel*) may have kept their own records and some of these are known, but in many cases they recorded the boy under his religious name with no reference to surname. The religious name may not be the name the boy was using in everyday life, and therefore even if there was a record, by later generations we may not be able to recognize it.

There was no ceremony whatsoever relating to the births of girls, and there is no independent record to look for. Marriage records will give the parents' names; censuses, burial records and grave inscriptions will give an age; wills may state a relationship – but in the end we may have to accept that we shall not get an exact statement of birth date.

The Sephardic Jews used surnames in the same manner as the Spanish and Portuguese Christians among whom they had lived. Their surnames are generally indistinguishable, but they use a range of Old Testament first names which were very little used by Catholics.

However, there was no long tradition of surname inheritance among Ashkenazim. Educated or middle-class or court Jews in Germany largely had surnames, but these were sometimes still at the stage of actually describing the holder. Thus sons or brothers might have different surnames which actually described them.

Jews who had been obliged to live in ghettoes often took or were given surnames as a condition of being allowed to live anywhere. This means that for families arriving in England it was not necessarily a psychological problem to abandon, translate or modify their surname. Nor were there any formalities in England that would make that difficult. The downside of that is that if your ancestors changed their name and the modern family have forgotten what the previous name was, there may be no documentary evidence to tell you.

Jewish gravestones usually include an inscription in Hebrew as well as in English. This often includes the name of the deceased expressed in terms of forename and father's forename. The father's forename is very unlikely to be given in the English inscription which, however, will include the surname.

Evidence of Jewish practice is proved by a couple having married in a synagogue, since synagogue marriages of Jews and non-Jews were never permitted. To repeat the point, this is a religious definition – not a racial or cultural one – and many non-Jews may have converted. In order to marry in a synagogue, it is necessary to have a certificate from the Beth Din (the office of the Chief Rabbi) declaring that you are clear to marry. These give birthplace and sometimes information about brothers.

The Beth Din holds case files of adoptions, conversions, divorces and also certificates of evidence for much of the 19th and 20th centuries. With the exception of the certificates of evidence, all other documents are confidential and information will only be supplied to those with a legitimate legal interest. The certificates of evidence were required by the Chief Rabbi to authorize marriages and they contain details of the applicant's date, age and place of birth and/or marriage abroad. The certificates often contain additional information to those issued by the Registrar General's Office and are particularly useful for tracing those who did not naturalize, where information about their origin or marriage abroad may not exist elsewhere. The Beth Din only accepts visits by prior appointment.

Further evidence of Jewish practice is given by membership of a Burial Society and the type of religious tradition is shown by which cemetery an individual was buried in. This is obviously most true in London, where there was a wide choice, and less true in places where the community was small.

Jews who lived far from the major centres of the community must have had to travel to get to religious services. If records give no indication of residence, you may not realize that your ancestors actually lived 20 or 30 miles from the synagogue.

The very large number of poor Jews who came into Britain in the years 1880–1914 galvanized prosperous established Jews to set up charities to deal with them. The anglicized Jews were afraid that poor Jews would frighten the ratepayers – exactly the same as the prosperous Huguenots had thought in the late 17th century. Many Jewish charities were set up for Jewish immigrants. The best known of these is probably the Jews' Temporary Shelter; its records are now in the London Metropolitan Archives. There were a few specifically Jewish schools, but many Jews attended the local state school and may have gone to an Anglican school.

Most immigrant Jews did not bother to naturalize, or not straightaway, as there was no particular advantage to this. However, in the next generation quite a few children brought into the country by their parents naturalized when they themselves were adult. Records are in the National Archives in series HO 1, but there is no religious aspect to this.

Tracing Jewish ancestry outside Britain has become immeasurably easier since 1990 and there are many useful links on the National Archives' website 'Moving Here'. For those families who have lived in the United Kingdom from before 1837, there are four magnificent collections, all now in the Society of Genealogists: The Darcy Hart Collection; The Hyamson Collection; The Mordy Collection; and The Colyer Ferguson Collection.

See also *My Ancestors were Jewish*, Charles Tucker (Society of Genealogists, 2005), publications of the Jewish Historical Society and *Shemot,* the journal of the Jewish Genealogical Society of Great Britain.

Chapter 8

South Asian cultures and faiths

by Abi Husainy
Record Specialist, The National Archives, Kew

South Asians began arriving in Britain in the 18th century. At that time, according to the historical journal *Past and Present* (no. 158, 1998), Indian weavers and other skilled labourers may have enjoyed a better standard of living than their British counterparts. Mirza Abu Taleb Khan, an Indian Muslim born in Lucknow who visited Ireland in 1800, took note of grim conditions in northern Europe: 'The poverty of peasants or common people in [Ireland] is such that the peasants of India are rich when compared to them.' This sense of comparative prosperity did not last, as India faced devastating economic setbacks and widespread famines in the 1830s and 1840s.

By the second half of the 19th century, several hundred South Asians had established roots in the British Isles, although many newcomers continued to return promptly to their native lands. As Britain had colonized India and Ceylon (Sri Lanka), South Asians came to this country to study or work, including thousands of Indian seamen known as Lascars (page 23). Lascars were predominantly Muslims from Bengal, Bombay, Karachi, the Punjab and the Madras port region of India.

More Muslims than Hindus came to Britain at this time. In explanation, historians have suggested that high-caste Hindus feared that by crossing the seas they could lose all connection with their religion and sacred places in their Indian homeland. Some devout Hindus criticized distant sea travel as a danger to the faith, though reform currents in the late 19th and early 20th century responded that the religion in ancient times had in fact many moral exemplars supporting seafaring activity.

The majority of the Lascars were Indians and Chinese, with a substantial sprinkling of Yemenis. The condition and treatment of the Lascars on the ships were harsh, and some of them eventually abandoned the seafaring life and made their way to British cities. Those who remained took jobs locally as street sweepers, hawkers, peddlers and servants. Many worked for the missionaries, while there were others who fell into destitution.

Certainly not all Asians who settled in Great Britain were seamen living in poor conditions. Professionals such as teachers, doctors, lawyers and businessmen also made an impact. Joseph Salter, a 19th-century Christian missionary in the Edgware Road area of London, travelled to Birmingham 'in search of the wandering Asiatic' in 1869, where he found a mixture of professionals, students and former seamen. Salter worked closely with the Lascar community for almost 40 years, including serving at the Strangers' Home for Destitute Lascars. This institution opened in Limehouse, London, in 1857; it was visited by 16,000 Lascars in 16 years.

In the 20th century, South Asians encountered obstacles to obtaining accommodation and had to take lower-paying jobs such as factory work and taxi driving, although many were educated and came from middle-class families in their country of origin. During the struggle to get established in British cities, they initially found it difficult to organize proper places of worship and thus relied on private houses. However, as the community grew in seaport towns such as Cardiff and Liverpool, as well as in London, members started arranging religious places to worship. Many also formed associations to make their political voice heard concerning Indian independence.

In the 19th century, Asians had encountered challenges when they tried to integrate, as their religions were often different from those of the society around them. Many converted to Christianity and took anglicized names, as they wanted to fit in and be accepted by the host community. The vast majority did not change their names legally.

This chapter mainly covers the period from the late 19th century to the 1960s and beyond, focusing on how South Asians founded religious organizations in Britain. It will explore how religious ceremonies around marriages and deaths were conducted, and where the relevant records for family historians are held in the UK, as well as in South Asian countries of origin.

Many of the records in the National Archives (and referred to in this chapter) show how successive governments sought to develop record systems for religions other than Christianity. There are many examples of individual cases – some of the most interesting ones feature here – but they are not a systematic record of everyone in the category.

New religions in Britain

The vast majority of the South Asian population who arrived in Britain from India came after Independence in 1947, and there were many later arrivals from Pakistan, Sri Lanka, Nepal and Bangladesh. Post-war arrivals also included Indian indentured labourers who had migrated to sugar-producing colonies during the colonial period and Indian workers who went to work in East Africa (Kenya and Uganda) in 1960. Most of them came from Hindu, Muslim, Sikh, Buddhist or Christian faiths, the last particularly strong among Anglo-Indians.

Seeking to preserve the customs and practices of their various faiths, these communities established their own religious organizations. As will be seen later, the more numerous Muslims began to build an institutional presence in the late 19th century, while other faith traditions gained momentum in the post-war period. Hindus, for example, founded the Sanatan Dharma Maha Sabha (a conservative temple organization). In London during November 1948, another Hindu current led by Swami Ghanananda opened the Ramakrishna Vedanta Centre. Similarly, Muslims have created numerous religious and cultural associations such as the East London Mosque and Islamic Centre, which grew from a small prayer room in 1910 to a fully fledged place of worship in 1941. The Jamiat-ul-Muslimin of London and Glasgow also helped create new centres of religious and community activity. The Sikhs meanwhile established their *gurdwaras* as centres for worship and fellowship. During 1958 in Smethwick, Birmingham, the first Guru Nanak Gurdwara opened at a Brass House Lane primary school; by 1961, the growing community purchased a church at 130 High Street and converted it into a permanent Sikh place of worship.

These religious frameworks and institutions have sometimes caused separations and fissures between Asians of different faiths, though they have also heightened unity within the individual religious groups. Any records created by these organizations are either deposited with local county record offices or held at the relevant institution itself.

For family historians it is important to understand the difficulties their ancestors went through to hold on to the customs of their culture and their religion. Before the 1950s, many Asians did not know the days for celebrating their religious festivals. They found out through newsletters or journals, or through friends and families of their community or organization, or relevant religious places. There was no ethnic minority media at that time via radio, television or internet. Many had no telephones. The religious places were thus a key source of communication for social and cultural news and for issues of worship. Therefore, it is important to understand how these communities established themselves and developed cultural networks. Records created by these places of worship may help in tracing family history in Britain.

Records of religious and cultural centres

There was a need for the South Asian community to have proper religious houses in which to practice religion. Initially the size of the community was too small to support many places of worship financially. According to the UK's national census of 1961, there were 50,000 Muslims and seven places of worship; 16,000 Sikhs, with three places of worship; and for the nation's 30,000 Hindus, only one place of worship. The intervening decades have seen prodigious growth in both population and places of worship. In the 2001 census, there were nearly 1,600,000 Muslims, with 614 places of worship; 340,000 Sikhs, with 193 places of worship; and 560,000 Hindus, with 109 places of worship.

While the practice of religion may have diminished overall in Britain, it remains a strong source of community and identity among many recent South Asian immigrants. For family historians, religious institutions are important not only as a way in which communities hold on to traditions, but also as places in which people may find new routes to integration in British society.

The creation of religious and cultural centres generated plenty of official documentation, and today the National Archives holds many records. Correspondence relating to the proposals to establish a Hindu temple and Indian Cultural Centre in London, for example, are in file DO 163/83, which also includes a report on the International Hindu Institute. Shree Hindu Vishva Mandir's plans for an Indian cultural centre in London, designed to propagate specialized aspects of Indian art and religion in Britain, are dated September 1964.

As noted earlier, many Hindus remained committed to the sacred places of India and hesitated at first to build permanent places of worship in Britain. The community rented places and looked for halls to celebrate special religious occasions throughout the year. In 1956 Indo-Caribbeans often rented Lambeth Town Hall in south London, for example, with services led by a priest from Guyana. Soon joined by immigrants from India, East Africa, and Mauritius, the Indo-Caribbeans worked with their co-religionists to form the Hindu Dharma Sabha in 1957, regarded as one of the first bodies to fight for the spiritual needs of Hindu newcomers to Britain. A very ecumenical North Indian rite prevailed, but elsewhere Gujaratis and Punjabis developed organizations favouring Hindu rites closer to their communities' various traditions.

Some anthropologists have hinted that Hindus who came from East Africa and the Caribbean had more tenuous ties with mother India, and they seemed to be over-represented in the early efforts to establish permanent temples. As Steven Vertovec, an Oxford academic, reflects in *The Hindu Diaspora*, the growth of permanent temples in the 1960s and 1970s often drew upon their assistance:

A Hindu Temple in Coventry that opened in 1967 is purported to be Britain's first. One temple after another was founded in rapid succession, often with the substantial contributions of wealthy Hindu businessmen. The tide of immigrants from East African countries in the late 1960s and early 1970s did much to hasten the organization of local Hindus and the establishment of temples, for they had gained useful experience in doing just those things during their prior experience of diaspora. Within ten years following the opening of the first temple, eighty-two Hindu temples across the country had been founded.

The Arya Samaj was an organization founded in 1875 in Mumbai to promote a spiritual revival of Hinduism and defence of Vedic wisdom. It spread among the South Asian diaspora in East Africa and East Asia during the early twentieth century, and in 1962 several figures associated with Arya Samaj created a society known as the Hindu Centre, London. Renting out St. Michael's Hall in Golders Green, the Arya Samaj then purchased separate facilities in 1968 and soon turned for leadership to the Vedic missionary Dr. Shruti Sheel Sharma. He had long experience in the West Indies including in Guyana and Surinam. In 1970 Arya Samaj established a new Vedic Mission in Hounslow where in the early days they rented the Alexandra Road School for their congregational meetings. A third Vedic Mission was set up at 387 High Street in Birmingham, several blocks down the road from the Sikh temple.

Meanwhile, Sikhs and Muslims had long pioneered the establishment of an institutional presence in Britain. The Khalsa Jatha, a religious society for Sikhs, was formed in Britain in 1908 at Putney, southwest London. In 1913 the Khalsa Jatha purchased the lease of 79 Sinclair Road, and has been based there since. Such centres proved a very important focus for communities seeking to establish themselves in Britain. They offered a forum to discuss everyday issues that arose when a secular world could appear to clash with religious beliefs – in the case of Sikhs, often related to concerns over the wearing of turbans and beards at work. Under certain circumstances and conditions, these were thought by British authorities to be a safety or hygiene hazard. The Metropolitan Police's debate on the wearing of turbans by Sikh officers is in file HO 287/1448, while a proposal to allow Sikh traffic wardens to wear turbans in place of caps is in HO 310/36.

In 1887 a successful lawyer, William Henry Quilliam, embraced Islam, changing his name to Sheikh Abdullah Quilliam. He returned from Morocco to Liverpool in 1889 to lead a small Muslim community; converts included his sons, prominent scientists and Quilliam's mother, who became known to local Muslims as Khadijah ('Mother of the Faithful'). In 1891, a rented house at 8 Brougham Terrace served as a prayer hall. Later the community purchased the rented property and also the units at 9–12, which became the Liverpool Muslim Institute. Up to a hundred Muslims could pray there, and the *khutbah* (sermon) was conducted in Arabic and English. The Institute also held courses for Muslims and non-Muslims in arts, science and law.

Quilliam also founded the Medina Home to care for local children and place them with Muslim foster families. With almost 2000 illegitimate births per year in Liverpool, pressures on the city's resources were acute. Quilliam founded a weekly journal called *The Crescent* that was published from 1893 to 1908 and also wrote *The Faith of Islam, an explanatory sketch of the tenets of the Moslem religion* (T. Dobb & Co., Liverpool, 1889). Some of these copies are held at the British Library.

The first Islamic mosque was built at Woking in 1889 by an Orientalist, Dr Gottlieb

Leitner. The cost of this mosque was donated by Indian Muslims, especially the wife of Shah Jahan, ruler of Bhopal in India, and hence it is called Shah Jahan Mosque. The first Imam was Khaja Kamal ud Din, a brilliant scholar and barrister from what is now Pakistan, who came to Richmond, Surrey, in 1912 and repaired and restored Woking Mosque. It was to become a social centre of British Islam and attracted some high-profile converts from the middle and upper classes.

In 1913 Khaja Kamal ud Din published the first issue of the journal *Muslim India and Islamic Review*. The following year he reversed the title to *The Islamic Review and Muslim India*, and by 1921 it was renamed simply *The Islamic Review*, Woking. In 1967 the journal assumed the final title of *The Islamic Review & Arab Affairs* before ceasing publication in the early 1970s. This journal, which includes occasional obituaries, was mainly aimed at presenting Islam to the Western world and to Muslims living in Britain and India. The British Library holds some copies of the journal for 1913, 1914 and 1919, while the School of Oriental and African Studies in London has a nearly complete set in its library. It is also available online at *www.wokingmuslim.org/work/islamic-review/index.htm*.

Files relating to Khaja Kamal ud Din's burial at Woking in 1933 are in the National Archives (HLG 45/95).

A Muslim cemetery was established in Brookwood, Woking, and the cemetery was bought by the British government during the Second World War to bury the Muslim soldiers who served among the Allied forces. The burial registers of this cemetery are held at the Surrey County Record Office at Woking. The correspondence between the War Office and the India Office relating to this, as well as an Ordnance Survey map showing the proposed location for the cemetery, is in the National Archives in WO 32/18578.

An Islamic Cultural Centre established in 1944 at Regent's Lodge site on the western boundary of Regent's Park, London, was to become the focus of Muslim religious activities in Britain. This site used to belong to the British crown, and was presented to the Muslim authorities in Britain by George VI on 21 November 1944. Several designs submitted by the Central London Mosque Trust were rejected by the Royal Fine Arts Commission and the Greater London Council as the minaret's height came into conflict with the North Terrace, a nearby building. In 1968 the Mosque Trust set up an international competition for an acceptable design. The London architect Sir Frederick Gibbard won the competition in 1969, receiving an award of £3,000. The construction of this mosque started in 1974 and finished in 1977. Correspondence relating to the acquisition of the Regent's Lodge site for a mosque is in WORK 16/1575–6 (1940–55), while that regarding the proposed erection of a central London mosque is in WORK 16/2236–7 (1963–71). Document references CRES 35/4909, 5193, CRES 57/194 and INF 6/1326 dated 1961 also relate to Regent's Park Mosque.

There are relatively few South Asian Christians in Britain, but they have gained more prominence in the Anglican Church through the rise of Bishop Michael Nazir-Ali, born in Pakistan and a current member of Britain's House of Lords. On the ground, a Methodist Church in Cowley Road, Oxford, has Punjabi-speaking services on Sundays that alternate with masses for the English-speaking local community. Records on South Asian Christians may be deposited at the local county record offices.

Parsees or Parsis

In the 1850s significant numbers of Parsees, or Parsis, arrived in Britain to pursue careers and to trade. They were originally Zoroastrians who fled from Persia due to Muslim religious persecution, and many took refuge in Africa and India. Those who went to India are called Parsees. In 1861, the Religious Society of Zoroastrians was founded in Britain, and it established a burial ground at Woking. Correspondence, designs and notes concerning the Wadia Mausoleum and the Parsee Cemetery in Woking are now held at the British Library (reference Mss Eur F216/82 – dated 1900–01).

Mixed and irregular marriages

Marriage laws and customs in India have varied from those in the UK, and South Asians were often unfamiliar with the laws of Britain. Many did not seek to violate British laws, but made mistakes in the beginning through ignorance of the British system. Participants often also lacked full knowledge of the consequences. For example, the Christian marriages of women of British nationality to Asian men that were undertaken in temples and mosques were considered illegal in the late 19th century and through the 1920s and 1930s – because these places of worship were not registered for the solemnization of marriages.

Marriage in such circumstances was regarded as an offence under Section 39 of the Marriage Act, 1836, and the priest and committee of the mosque or temple would be accountable for any irregularities. The Marriage Act proscribed certain marriages celebrated without the proper formalities outlined in the legislation. There are a few criminal investigation department case files that are held at the National Archives in record series RG 48, covering the period 1900–70.

For example, RG 48/2934–6 gives examples of irregular marriages of Muslims between 1965 and 1971, and RG 48/2937–42 those of Sikhs between 1962 and 1968. Correspondence relating to marriages solemnized according to Muslim law is in HO 144/17244, covering the period from 1905 to 1933.

This document contains files on Clara Casey from the city of Salford, Manchester. She was married to Mohammed Ben Belkhassam, a Moroccan acrobat, at the Liverpool Mosque on 13 March 1905. The marriage was conducted according to the Muslim rites and took place with the consent of her parents, although the girl was a minor at the time of marriage. They travelled to Morocco where a few months later the couple had disagreements, and Belkhassam struck her. Casey wrote to her parents about the ill-treatment. Her parents contacted the British consulate at Tangier, who investigated, and Belkhassam was sent to prison while she travelled back to England. This case attracted the attention of the Home Office and the General Register Office, who investigated where and how the marriage was conducted. The document includes a copy of a despatch from HM Consul at Tangier concerning the treatment of Clara Casey by Belkhassam, as well as their marriage certificate from the Liverpool Mosque and correspondence from Sheikh Abdullah Quilliam.

It also includes two more cases, that of Selim Hnowy – a Turk who married Miss Emily Bostock on 22 March 1902 – and that of Mohamed Amin Rifaat Zada, an Egyptian also married to an Englishwoman. Both couples went through the Muslim form of marriage before Sheikh Abdullah Quilliam of Liverpool.

There was hostility towards and disapproval of mixed marriages by British society, and they were often sensationalized. Occasionally a mixed marriage made big news in the local newspapers. The general opinion was that mixed marriages between Englishwomen and non-Christians brought misery and distress to the women, although some of the marriages proved successful.

Concern was also expressed – and recorded – by the various Superintendent Registrars in India about the marriages of Englishwomen with Hindus or Muslims. The marriages were valid in England but not in India where there was no *lex loci* (a Latin term referring to the 'law of the place' where an action was undertaken). In other words, Indian authorities did not feel compelled to uphold legal actions in another part of the world. Instead, every person was governed by the law of his personal status. For example, a Muslim man is entitled to have four wives and is not bound in religion by any restrictive covenant that he may have entered into with his first wife. A few case files containing details of such marriages, with their marriage certificates, are held in the National Archives series RG 41 and RG 48.

A particularly interesting case can be found in RG 48/216 relating to a Muslim man, Mir Anwaruddin, and his English wife. After marrying her in England in 1913, Anwaruddin sought to divorce his wife through a *talaq*, recognized by many Muslims as a formal declaration of divorce. However, the Divisional Court later went on record to reject this procedure, as it was not a legal form of divorce in Britain. Anwaruddin protested that his first wife, Ruby Pauline Hudd, had deserted him, and the British courts were both preventing him from divorcing and denying him the right to marry his second British wife according to Muslim procedure. Their divorce case files are held under document references J 77/1119 (case no. 3971), J 77/1126 (case no. 4194) and J77/1258 (case no. 8351).

Hindu law of marriage

Divorces, whether in Britain or abroad, were (and are still) often problematic where different faiths and cultures were involved. As the registrars of the register offices were often not satisfied with the evidence provided by the parties, such proceedings produced plenty of official records, some of which are now preserved at the National Archives. One document, RG 48/216, includes correspondence from the General Register Office, Somerset House, London WC2 relating to the Hindu law of marriage. It was requested by R. Bridger, Superintendent Registrar, Register Office,

Hampstead Town Hall, Haverstock Hill NW3, in connection with the case of a Hindu man, K.S. Deo (the Zamindar of Jarda), who had a wife in India and wanted to marry an Englishwoman in this country. His claim was that he had divorced his wife in accordance with Hindu custom. This document includes some information on Hindu law. According to this, marriage is regarded as a sacrament and an indissoluble union. Divorce, therefore, is an unknown concept in Hindu society. The law allows a man to have several wives, and it forbids a woman to marry again even after the death of her first husband. Theoretically, the practice of polygamy renders dissolution of marriage unnecessary for the husband, and the prohibition of the second marriage of the woman renders divorce useless for the wife. A Hindu man may also marry again, without the consent of his wife, if his first marriage was not conducted according to the Hindu religion.

Though sacred Hindu law does not overtly allow for the dissolution of a marital union, divorce and marriage of a divorced wife was carried out in some cases by custom. According to P.K. Virdi's analysis in *The Grounds for Divorce in Hindu and English Law* (Motilal Banarsidass, 1972), 'When it is impossible to act up to the precepts of sacred law, it becomes necessary to adopt a method founded on reasoning, because custom decides everything and overrules the sacred law ... the Vedas, the *shmitris* and the practices of good men are the sources of law.' For Hindus a customary divorce features mutual consent and a letter of release known as the *chor chitti* in which the husband consents to grant the wife her freedom. Other mechanisms are also employed to help when relationships fragment. In Hindu law, a type of separation classified as desertion (*tyaga*) is regarded as distinct from divorce as the marital tie is not fully terminated.

Many people establishing new lives for themselves in Britain did form new relationships, which could be problematic if there were existing liaisons in their countries of origin. An example in the National Archives is the case of Dhansukhbhai Lalkibhai Patel and Savitaben Patel, who sought in the 1960s to get married in the UK despite previous marriages to other people in India; both of them claimed to be divorced. The file (RG 48/2568) includes their respective divorce papers from India and confirming court documents from the advocates in Bombay and Surat; there is also a letter from the legal adviser of the High

Commission of India dated 27 February 1961 testifying that they cannot certify the validity of the respective divorces. It includes the record of a community-approved customary divorce and a copy notice of marriage without licence between the parties.

In cases such as these, where there was evidence a man has or had a wife back in India (or a woman a husband), the British state required proof that the spouse had either died or that there had been a legally recognized divorce. Lacking such evidence, the Registrar General might decide whether a statutory declaration of the facts would be acceptable in order for the Superintendent General to accept notice of marriage.

Another National Archives record, RG 48/2603, contains files taking up the case of a house at Moss Side, 15 Monton Street, Manchester. It had become a Sikh temple, but had not been registered to carry out marriages. As a result, Bhi Mehar Singh Pardesi, Secretary and High Priest of the Sikh temple, faced legal action from the Manchester Crown Court in 1956 for carrying out weddings. As becomes clear from the file, the Superintendent General must receive proper notification of an intended marriage. The file also contains newspaper cuttings of the *Manchester Evening Chronicle* (13 June 1961) and a marriage certificate of Sardar Singh and Rani Bhai Rattan.

The records of non-Christian marriages and divorces contain many cases that do not conform to the conventional routines of British jurisprudence. These episodes can help social scientists and legal scholars confront many of the peculiarities of British traditions, while also helping family historians to identify the ways newcomers adjusted to their adopted homes. These court records provide some of the most vivid testimony of the cultural encounters and

---

Did you know?

The naming system among the Sikhs and most other Indians is traditionally very different from the practices of Western countries. 'Kaur' and 'Devi' form part of a Sikh female's name and indicate gender, while 'Singh' is part of a male's name. 'Kaur' and 'Devi' are normally suffixes used after the woman's first name. Generally, women in India did not use their husband's surname, and there is no family surname at all used in the Sikh community. Now the system has changed to become more in line with Western practice. Document reference RG 48/2374 (in the National Archives) includes an example of a birth certificate, which shows Kaur written as the mother's maiden name.

misunderstandings between South Asians and native Britons.

Hindu and Sikh burials in inland waterways

When a Sikh or Hindu dies, traditionally the body is cremated on an open-air pyre. As it is not permitted in this country to cremate in an open area, cremations are carried out in the local crematoria. The pulverized ashes and flowers are ceremoniously scattered in flowing water, and the reciting of prayers accompanies the event. In the 1940s to 1960s ashes were taken back to India by relatives, to be placed in the Ganges, Jumna or other rivers. In some cases, bodies were sent back to India and cremated there. In other cases, however, cremated remains of Sikhs and Hindus were cast upon the River Thames or other inland waterways as part of a religious burial ceremony – which was in fact an offence against various British acts and bye-laws. Nevertheless, because of the importance of this, bereaved families approached local police stations with requests to cast cremated remains of relatives upon moving rivers. It is possible that the records may be kept at the relevant police stations. If those living nearby protested against these practices, they may have done so in local newspapers.

Associations and societies

South Asian immigrants in Britain have formed different types of associations. One example is the Pakistan Welfare Association, established in the 1950s. Another, the Indian Association (Bharatiya Mandala), was formed in Bradford during October 1959; by 1969 it owned its own premises. Indian students who were studying in Edinburgh founded the Edinburgh Indian Association in 1883, and some of the correspondence relating to the legal cases is held by the Edinburgh University Library, Special Collections at George Square, Edinburgh EH8 9LJ.

The National Indian Association has records relating to the welfare of Indian students in England between 1870 and 1949. They are available in the British Library, Asia, Pacific and Africa Collections.

Many of these associations helped their communities to deal with the problems arising from the host society, such as immigration, racism and work-related matters. They also organized community events and set up community classes or schools to teach South Asian languages to their children who were born in this country. It is probable that the records of those Asian immigrants who were contributors and members of these associations may be kept at the appropriate local county record offices.

Coventry is the birthplace of the Indian Workers Association, an organization founded shortly before the outbreak of the Second World War by a handful of Indian students and professional Indian men. Among its main purposes, it sought to prepare Indian workers to take part in the struggle for independence upon their return to India, to promote social and cultural activities between the Indian and British people and to provide for the general welfare of Indian workers. According to the Home Office's Special Branch report of 30 November 1943, the Indian Workers Association was also known as the Indian Workers Union, while the Hindustani Mazdur Sabha was founded by a Madrasi named V.S.S. Sastryn in Birmingham in 1941.

Birmingham City Archives holds the Indian Workers Association records, and a document at the National Archives, HO 45/25460, gives some biographical details of editors of the Indian Workers Association newspaper *Azad Hind*, a bilingual monthly in Punjabi and Urdu. The British Library, Oriental and India Office Collections hold India, Pakistan and Burma

Association records in MSS Eur F 158.

Many Asian immigrants who were compelled to migrate to this country in the 1960s started newsagent businesses, and their details may be available from the National Federation of Retail Newsagents at the following address:

Yeoman House
Sekforde Street
London EC1R 0HF
Tel: 0207 253 4225
Fax: 0207 250 0927
Website: *www.nfrn.org.uk*

Film societies grew up across Britain during the 1950s. In various towns with a concentration of Indo-Pakistani immigrants, the communities established film societies, including four in the Birmingham region. Some commercial cinema entrepreneurs would feature Indian and Pakistani movies on weekends and holidays. Elsewhere, private film societies benefited from the organizing drive of tight-knit family networks among immigrants.

The Eastern Film Society was founded in January 1956 in Wolverhampton in the West Midlands, and many Asians living in this area belonged to it. The main objective of these societies was to give social life and cultural entertainment to the community. The first generation of Asians were very proactive, making extra efforts to teach their children about their cultural and religious heritage.

Asian newspapers

Different newspapers or magazines published by the various Asian communities or associations can prove invaluable sources of information about Asian people and events. So can newsletters and annual reports published by the mosques, temples, gurdwaras and churches for their individual communities. All of these may be held at the county record offices, at local reference libraries or at the places of worship themselves. It is also worth checking local and national newspapers for obituaries and other articles that may contain interesting details.

Marriages and deaths of those from the Asian community were normally announced in local Asian newspapers. They often also appear in the national newspapers of their country of origin, in the hope of notifying friends and relatives in towns and villages.

Records in other countries

To complete research into family history, it is important to consult not only British records, but also records available in the immigrant's country of origin. It is thus necessary to define more precisely where the family came from. According to Rashmi Desai in *Indian immigrants in Britain* (from file HO 344/194 in the National Archives), 'Almost all South Asian immigrants come from the two traditional areas of emigration, the Punjab and Gujarat. The chief regions are the Jullunder and Hoshiarpur districts of the Punjab and Central and Southern Gujarat. Pakistanis come from the Punjab area of West Pakistan, the Mirpur district of Kashmir and Sylhet in East Pakistan. Since 1960 some Gujaratis have come to the United Kingdom from East and Central Africa.'

The recent political geography of India and Pakistan must be borne in mind, as East and West Pakistan State was not created until August 1947. One should consider asking the following questions:

- If your ancestors were born in the old Indian territories that are now in Pakistan, do you know which states they came from?

- Were they born in East Pakistan, which became Bangladesh in 1972?
- Did they opt to migrate to Pakistan from India during Partition?
- Did they migrate from East Pakistan to West Pakistan for employment? Did they then proceed to Britain?
- Did they choose to migrate directly to England or first from India to Pakistan then to this country?
- Were they indentured labourers from Tamil Nadu (Madras Presidency, later Madras State) who migrated for work under British rule to Sri Lanka (Ceylon)?

This section gives some basic guidance on what type of information may be available in the South Asian countries. The information given in this section is collected from the community, the High Commissions and from the National Archives of India.

India

The National Archives of India was established in Calcutta in 1891 as the Imperial Record Department. Since 1947, the National Archives of India has established four regional offices, at Bhopal, Jaipur, Bhubaneswar and

Pondicherry. They may be contacted through the following address:

National Archives of India
Janpath
New Delhi-110001
India
Tel.:   00 91-11-233834 36
Fax no.:   00 91-11-233841 27
Email: *archives@nic.in*

Births and deaths in India are normally registered with the local Municipality Office, and the registers passed to the District Registrar's Office. Deaths are only registered when there is a legal case, if the deceased has left land, if they had a bank account, through a claim to a pension or if the death occurred through an accident or murder, etc. Prosperous families normally announce deaths in national and local newspapers. *The Hindu*, the national and regional newspaper, has an obituary column. It started in 1878 as a weekly and it became a daily in 1889.

Marriage records of Goans and Anglo-Indians are held at the various churches. Muslim marriages (*Nikah Nama*) are normally recorded in the local mosque registers, but not all the

records have survived or actively been con-
served. If the marriage was conducted legally
in a register office, the relevant records are
held at the local Marriage Registration Office.
Some temples in India keep Hindu marriage
registers, but they are not complete records.
Prosperous families announced marriages in
the local or national newspapers.

Hindu pilgrimage and marriage records
It may also be possible to trace records of
Hindu pilgrimages and marriages. The
Genealogical Society (GSU) of Utah, USA, has
microfilmed Hindu pilgrimage records for
Haridwar and several other Hindu pilgrimage
centres. These records were created by
priests (pandits) located at each site who
recorded the name, date, hometown and purpose of visit for each pilgrim. These records
were grouped according to family and ancestral home. The holdings of the GSU include
Haridwar, Kurukshetra, Pehowa, Chintpurni,
Jawalapur and Jawalamukhi.

The GSU has also microfilmed Maithil
Brahmin genealogical records – which establish degrees of relationship between prospec-
tive brides and grooms to determine whether
a potential marriage is prohibited. There are

also Islamic marriage records for:

Meerut (Uttar Pradesh): Qazi-Muslim marriage records, 1881–1982

Bulandshahr (Uttar Pradesh): Qazi-Muslim marriage records, 1921–55.

Microfilm copies of these records have been deposited at the National Archives of India for access.

Bangladesh

Registering births, marriage and deaths is not mandatory in Bangladesh, and in rural areas some people did not register at all. Relevant records may be held at the City Council or Municipal Corporation of each town.

During Partition in 1947 a successful attempt was made to divide archival material equally between East and West Bengal. In 1971, similar attempts were made to claim material relevant to East Bengal (East Pakistan) from the Pakistan authorities. However, not all the records were transferred to Bangladesh.

The National Archives of Bangladesh holds the district records, proceedings, secretariat records, the Dhaka Divisional Commissioner's Office records, old newspapers, Government

Gazettes, press cuttings, old maps and gazettes and printed correspondence files from Calcutta, all of which were transferred in 1947. These are not a complete collection, however. The address for further research is:

Bangladesh National Library and Archives
32 Justice Sayed Mahbub Murshed Sarani
Sher-e-Bangla Nagar (Agargaon)
Dhaka 1207
Bangladesh
Tel.:   00 88-02-9129992
Fax: 00 88-02-9118704
Email: *nabdirector@gmail.com*

For further advice on family history research in Bangladesh, please contact the National Archives of Bangladesh.

Pakistan
In most of Pakistan, the reporting of births is not mandatory, and finding records in rural areas can be a difficult task. Elsewhere, there have been some major losses of records, most notably in 1948 when fire engulfed the vast majority of collections on vital statistics held by the municipality of Karachi.

The Registrar of Births and Deaths or the

Director of Health Statistics in a municipality are the most likely sources for many types of birth records, if they exist. In the rural regions, try consulting the union council, district council or district health officer. The reality is that many births are registered relatively late in childhood, and a diligent researcher should thus consider consulting the school records. For many Pakistanis, the principal or headmaster provides school or matriculation certificates, which also confirm the date of birth and the father of the pupil.

One of the trickier aspects of searches for Pakistani names is the variety of combinations and spellings. Some individuals change their names through an announcement in the newspaper. In the case of very old citizens and rural dwellers, it is common to find only the year of birth and no day or month.

The Registrar of Births and Deaths in a municipality or union council is an obvious source for the recording of deaths. Cantonment boards in cities can also issue death certificates. However, it should be stressed that the registration of deaths is inconsistently carried out in many areas, and searches may not be successful.

Muslims need to register their marriages

with the Nikah Registrar, who receives an appointment from the municipality, Panchayat committee and cantonment board or union council. The marriage certificate, known as the *Nikah Nama*, is written in Urdu, though a translation authenticated for accuracy may accompany the document.

For non-Muslims, including Christians, Hindus and Parsis, it is usually the case that church or temple leaders must register the marriage with local authorities. If non-Muslims desire to make their marriage part of the civil record, they can later have certificates prepared that are witnessed by magistrates, a procedure in accordance with the Christian Marriage Act of 1892.

With the exception of Azad Kashmir, all zones of Pakistan make divorce subject to forms of arbitration. In Azad Kashmir, some still practice the 'bare *talaq*' – a form of divorce in which a husband can sever a relationship with a triple declaration of the phrase, 'I divorce thee'. The oral quality of the 'bare *talaq*' decree may make a paper trail more difficult to find in Azad Kashmir.

Civil courts can grant Christians a divorce in Pakistan, and copies of a specific case ruling can be obtained from the court.

For further advice on family history research in Pakistan, please contact the National Archives of Pakistan. The details are as follows:

National Archives of Pakistan
Adminstrative Block N
Pakistan Secretariat
Islamabad
Pakistan
Tel.:   00 92-51-9202044
Fax: 00 92-51-9206349

The Pakistan Genealogy Forum (*http://genforum.genealogy.com/pakistan*) also contains useful information for those researching their family tree and may be of interest.

Sri Lanka
A Sri Lankan genealogical forum where one can share family history information is available through www.genealogy.com. The web address is *www.genforum.genealogy. com/sri-lanka*. The National Archives of Sri Lanka holds:

- Land settlement records (1867–1900)
- Genealogical records (18th century)
- Birth details on palm leaves (1806–12)
- Voters registers (1965–92)

- Sinhala newspapers (1862–1976)
- English newspapers (1832–1976)
- Tamil newspapers (1864–1976)

These are invaluable sources for family historians. The address is:

National Archives of Sri Lanka
PO Box 1414
7 Reid Avenue
Colombo 7
Sri Lanka
Tel.:   00 94 1 694523/ 00 94 1 696917
Fax: 00 94 1 694419
Email: *narchive@slt.lk*

Information about the census records of Sri Lanka can be obtained from this address:

Information Unit
Department of Census & Statistics
PO Box 563, Colombo 07
Sri Lanka
Tel.:   00 94-011-268217 6
Email: *dgensus@sltnet.lk*

Sources of information

With substantial numbers of Asian immigrants

migrating to the UK during the 1950s, the community soon recognized that better solutions were needed to practice their varied religions and cultures. More recently, the government's efforts at multiculturalism have helped newer arrivals to feel more comfortable in pursuing their traditions, while also raising awareness of Britain's diverse heritage. More of the nation's archives are listing online catalogues with increasing amounts of documentation about the South Asian community. It is important to check the Access to Archives website at *www.a2a.org.uk*, and also to explore the appropriate local county record office websites. For guidance on how to find South Asian family history, please check the MovingHere website at *www.movinghere.org.uk/galleries/ roots/asian/asian.htm*.

There is still much work to be done in understanding the history of recent immigrants to Britain. It will take determined efforts by archivists, professional historians and amateur family biographers to recover this remarkable part of the nation's transformation.

Finding out more

As many organizations and county record

offices have come forward to celebrate the presence of South Asians in the UK, several useful websites have been created which give information on cultural events, festivals, arts, music and photographs. They also describe holdings that may be relevant to the history of South Asians in this country. These resources can be helpful in tracing information about individuals who played a part in building South Asian communities and institutions in the UK.

Oxford Centre for Hindu Studies
   http://www.ochs.org.uk/research/hindu_archive.html
Oxford Centre for Islamic Studies
   http://www.oxcis.ac.uk/
Centre of South Asian Studies: University of Cambridge
   http://www.s-asian.cam.ac.uk
Moving Here
   http://www.movinghere.org.uk
Oriental and India Office Collections: The British Library
   www.bl.uk
Caribbean Studies and the history of Black and Asian peoples in the UK
   http://www.casbah.ac.uk/

Anglo Sikh Heritage Trail
http://www.asht.info/
Imperial War Museum, Photograph Archive
http://www.iwm.org.uk/collections/photos.htm
Access to Archives
http://www.a2a.org.uk/
Bedfordshire and Luton Archives and Records
Service - Sources for Records relating to Ethnic
Minority Groups; Young Indians' Association
and South Asian Christian Association
http://www.bedfordshire.gov.uk/Resources
/PDF/E/Ethnic%20Sources.pdf
Record Office for Leicestershire
http://www.leics.gov.uk/museums/records/
index.htm
London Metropolitan Archives
http://www.cityoflondon.gov.uk/Corporation/
*leisure_heritage/libraries_archives_museums_*
galleries/lma/lma.htm
Birmingham City Archives
Photographs; Asian peoples; Cultural events;
Festivals; Sikhism
Photographs by Sangeeta Redgrave (Diwali –
the Hindu Festival of Lights)
Photographs by Ghazala Saddique (A Pakistani
Celebration – Lokmela) and Photographs by
Sukhvinder Singh Ubhi
The Dyche Collection *c.*1920–1980

Asian peoples; African-Caribbean peoples; Photographs
http://www.birmingham.gov.uk/Generate Content?
Ahmed Iqbal Ullah Race Relations Archive
http://www.racearchive.org.uk
South Asian Diaspora Literature and Arts Archive
http://www.salidaa.org.uk/salidaa/site/Home
North West Film Archive Commission
http://www.nwfa.mmu.ac.uk
AAVAA (African and Asian Visual Artists' Archive)
http://www.uel.ac.uk/aavaa/
North West Film Archive Commission
http://www.nwfa.mmu.ac.uk
Black and Asian Theatre
http://theatremuseum.vam.ac.uk/eduindex.htm

Chapter 9

Sources and records

This chapter describes most of the documentary sources for tracing the religious aspects of family history, particularly emphasizing those at the National Archives.

The records of the National Archives are primarily those of the state, or those that the state has taken into its keeping. Many of them have a religious aspect or were gathered because the state was interested in aspects of religion. Others are really about money which the Church was collecting but reporting to the state.

Some of this material has been taken from Stella Colwell's excellent *Dictionary of Genealogical Sources in the Public Record Office* (1992), but all appears in the National Archives catalogue. Informative leaflets are available on many sources, either in paper form or downloadable. As this book is concerned with tracing family history, a number of sources have been disregarded because they are not about names.

The National Archives has a system of letters and abbreviations which refer to the major record series. These are used as part of the documents' identification number, for example SP for State Papers or RG for Registrar General. The short forms are used throughout the following sections.

Anglican clergy

Certificates of institution to benefices between 1544 and 1912 are in E 331; lists of presentations to livings between 1829 and 1950 are in C 247. Committee for Plundered Ministers 1642–53 is in SP 22; relinquishments of holy orders (since 1870) is in J 18. Preferments and resignations of clergy from 1665 to 1986 are in the *London Gazette*. Most other material relates to payments of first fruits and tenths.

Army

Chaplains were attached to all regiments and regimental returns of baptisms and marriages are with the Office of National Statistics. There are many birth, baptism, marriage and death certificates from 1755 to 1902 in WO 42. Marriages between 1811 and 1872, and deaths between 1835 and 1888, are in WO 32/8920; official notifications of marriages from 1799 to 1882 are in WO 25/3239–45. These relate to the families of officers. Dates of marriage also appear in the lists of officers on half-pay or retired in WO 25/744–8. Royal Garrison Regiment officers' services, including details of marriages from 1901 to 1905, are in WO 19. Marriages (also births and deaths) of families of Army personnel overseas between 1627 and 1958 are in RG 33, indexed in RG 43.

Assizes

Many people came before the Assizes for matters religious in origin, but cases were only concerned with contravention of state law. From 1559 to 1778, for example, it was 'death for a priest to breathe the air of England'. Many religious preachers and pamphleteers were also tried for sedition.

Association Oath Rolls

In 1696 a plot was made to assassinate William III, and in its aftermath people were required to declare their support for the Protestant Succession. The Association Oath Rolls in C 213 record this; it was basically a confirmation of political allegiance, but also shows the religious attitudes of the signatories. There are some useful lists from particular religious groups, for example Baptist ministers (C 213/170); London Dissenters (C 214/9); Quakers at Colchester (C 213/473).

See *The Hearth Tax and other Stuart tax lists and the Association Oath Rolls*, Jeremy Gibson (Federation of Family History Societies, 1985 and later editions).

Attorneys

Oaths of Catholics between 1790 and 1836 and affirmations of Quakers between 1831 and 1842 are in CP 10 and E 3.

Births and baptisms

The National Archives has a few Anglican baptism registers, mostly relating to communities abroad. Look first in series RG 4–8.

Many birth and baptism registers were handed into public keeping by 1857 and are also in series RG 4–8. They mostly relate to Nonconformists, but include records of smaller foreign congregations. The Nonconformists had lobbied for this for a long time and wanted to hand their records in.

The registers of Dr Williams's Library (from 1742) are in RG 4/4666–76, with parchment certificates in RG 5. Those of the Wesleyan Metropolitan Registry (dating from 1817) are in

RG 4, and are indexed in RG 4/4680.

Comparatively few other records are known, so that it is customary to say 'All Nonconformist registers...'. However, the registers are those which were in existence at the time. We have no way of knowing what records there had been of chapels which have closed, or what chapels had never kept any registers.

Some baptism certificates from London parishes (1693 to 1826) are in KB 101/26. There are also certificates of marriage between 1744 and 1829 and burial from 1721 to 1831.

See *Using Baptism Records for Family Historians,* Pauline Litton (Federation of Family History Societies, 1996).

Chantries

Chantry surveys were made by the Crown Commissioners in 1545 and 1547 and give, among other information, the founder's name. Certificates are held in E 301, and those for the Duchy of Lancaster in DL 38. Warrants for pensions of dissolved chantries, 1548, are held in E 301.

Charities

Descriptive lists of deeds establishing charities and appointing trustees from 1812 to 1875 are in J 19, and from 1841 to 1953 in TS 18. Some have a religious motivation or object.

Church lands

Bargain and sales of church lands between 1650 and 1660 are enrolled on the Close Rolls in C 54.

Church school applications for government funding

In the mid-19th century, church schools were entitled to apply for state funding. The application forms in ED 7 supply information about the foundation, buildings and the subjects taught, but they also give the curriculum vitae of the teachers, including their place of birth, where they had been trained and the schools at which they had previously taught.

The Civil War and the Commonwealth

This was not technically about religion, but almost all Catholics supported the king and were therefore on the losing side. The Committee for Compounding with Delinquents was concerned with assessing the income, goods and lands of royalists with a view to assessing how much should be sequestrated (taken away). The records always say if the people under investigation were Catholic (recusants) as well as royalists (delinquents). Religion was much at the forefront of people's minds at this period, and a great deal of anecdotal material arises in all the State Paper (SP) series of the period.

Baptists, Presbyterians, Congregationalists and others were, in principle, on the winning side, so there are no records of them as delinquents. However, they did disagree fairly seriously with each other, and many individuals appear in local records as troublemakers.

The majority of these and the other groups of the time were not interested in the genealogical records sought by family historians. There are only a few registers of baptism this early in series RG 4 at the National Archives. However, many Quaker records of the period have survived (see below).

Coroners' records

Investigations into mysterious deaths may mention religion when it was connected, either directly – as in accusations of witchcraft – or indirectly, for example as the subject of the dispute in which the deceased died.

See *Coroners' Records in England and Wales*, Jeremy Gibson and Colin Rogers (Federation of Family History Societies, 1997).

Death and burial

A number of non-parochial burial registers are among the records in class RG 4. These include those from the Nonconformist burying ground in Bunhill Fields in London, as well as some other large early cemeteries.

See *Using Death and Burial Records for Family Historians*, Lilian Gibbens (Federation of Family History Societies, 1997).

Divorce

Before 1857 a private Act of Parliament was needed to obtain a divorce – see C 89 and C 204. A marriage could be ended by the ecclesiastical courts. From 1858 divorce was a state matter; records are in J 77, J 78 and TS 29. Depending on circumstances, an account may be found in local or national newspapers.

Many matrimonial disputes came to court without divorce. See instances between 1609 and 1834 in DEL 1, DEL 2, DEL 7, PCAP 1 and PCAP 3. Memoranda are in KB 29; background between 1536 and 1701 in KB 27, and between 1701 and 1857 in KB 28.

Doctor Williams's Library

A birth registry for Nonconformists from 1742 to 1837 is in RG 4 and 5.

Ecclesiastical causes

Writs were issued for the arrest of (some) people who had been excommunicated. Those from 1272 to 1701 are in KB 27; and those between 1702 and 1911 in KB 28. The Court of High Commission for Ecclesiastical Causes (1583–1641) was set up to investigate offences against the Acts of Supremacy and Uniformity; records are in SP 16.

Excommunication

Excommunication had legal and financial consequences as well as religious ones. Significations of excommunications from 1220 are in the National Archives in C 85. They give details of residence, occupation, paternity and offence, and are in Latin. Those from Elizabeth I's reign to Victoria's are in C 207, with a card index by diocese. Enrolments of writs to enforce excommunications are on the Controlment Rolls from 1330 to 1843 in KB 29, and from 1844 to 1880 in KB 5. Subsequent proceedings are in the Coram Rege Rolls from 1272 to 1701 in KB 27, and the Plea Rolls from 1702 to 1911 in KB 28.

There is separate material for Cheshire in CHES 38.

Fleet registers

These, together with those of other clandestine marriages, all in London, are in RG 7.

Foreign churches in England

Details of these are found in a subdivision of the non-parochial registers in series RG 4–8. They include Walloon, French, Dutch, German, Swiss, Russian and Greek congregations, but no non-Christians.

Foreign registers

These relate to baptisms, marriages and burials of British people abroad over varying periods of time. They are almost all in the RG and FO series. Search the catalogue under the name of the country that interests you.

Forfeited estates

Many Catholics suffered as Jacobites, but the crime was political not religious. See FEC 1 and FEC 2.

Grants of advowson

Details of these, the right to present to a living – that is, the right to appoint an Anglican clergyman – are in C 66. These appear in the patent rolls each time someone is presented.

Graves and tombstones

Copies of records, sometimes with plans and inscriptions relating to gravestones and tombs which have been removed, are in RG 37.

Land tax

Catholics were supposed to pay double, and records appear particularly in E 181 and E 182.

Lay subsidies

Foreigners were required to pay double the rate of lay subsidy (a tax based on the value of lands and possessions). From 1625 to 1660 the same rule was applied to Catholics ('because they are foreigners at heart') and records appear in E 179. See *Tudor and Stuart Tax Lists*, Jeremy Gibson (Federation of Family History Societies, 1985).

Lenten certificates

These are concerned with enquiries about those who had killed or eaten meat during Lent. Returns for the City of London from 1593 to 1641 are in C 265. Licences and presentments relating to selling meat in taverns and cookshops in the City of London are in C 203; victuallers' bonds are in E 180.

Marriage allegations/licences

The records give no clue as to the religious opinions of the parties. Having a licence was often convenient but never compulsory, and earlier Puritans or later dissenters who disliked the system could have the banns read. The system did not operate during the Commonwealth period. See *Bishops' Transcripts and Marriage Licences, Bonds and Allegations*, Jeremy Gibson (Federation of Family History Societies, 4th edition, 1997).

Marriages

In 1653 a system of civil marriage was established in accordance with the beliefs of many Puritans. In many cases the registrars used the parish register. There are no separate records.

Between 1754 and 1837 Nonconformists all married in the Church of England, with the sole exception of Quakers. Jews were also free to marry according to their own forms, but they were not, of course, Nonconformists. Among the pre-1754 registers for ordinary English meetings there are only two registers of marriage, both for fairly short periods.

However, the non-parochial registers in classes RG 4–8 include the Fleet Registers – many hundreds of notebooks relating to marriages (and some baptisms) which took place within the Liberties of the Fleet in central London before 1753. There are also registers for Mayfair Chapel, the Mint and King's Bench Prisons.

It is thought that about one-sixth of London couples were married in the Fleet in the 1740s as well as very many couples from the Home Counties. However, these were Anglican ministers marrying cheaply and fairly informally, and it is not likely that many Nonconformists went there for conscience's sake.

See *Using Marriage Records for Family Historians*, Pauline Litton (Federation of Family History Societies, 1996).

Monks

Files of warrants for pensions between 1536 and 1539 and 1552 to 1553 are in E 101 and SP 5 (these include immorality charges).

Naturalization and denization

The records for cases between 1509 and 1800 in HO 1 have been published by the Huguenot Society. Later records (same series) are available online. The Oath Roll of Naturalization for Protestant Refugees from 1708 and after is in E 169/86; accompanying sacrament certificates are in E 196/10.

Non-parochial registers

Authenticated registers of births, baptisms, marriages and burials, mostly to 1837 but a few to 1858, are in RG 4. Unauthenticated registers are in RG 8. (There is nothing doubtful about the entries, but they missed the deadline to be accepted as legal evidence. Non-parochial registers include Catholic registers for the Northeast.) Records in RG 4–8 are now online.

Registers including the British Lying In Hospital in Endell Street, Holborn, London are in RG 8; Royal Chapels are in RG 8.

Oath Rolls

These mostly relate to the Oaths of Loyalty (to the monarch) and Supremacy (to the monarch as head of the Church of England). Many Anglicans were required to take these as a condition of employment, and it was also necessary to present a certificate that they had taken Anglican communion within the previous year. They were thus standard and entirely unproblematic for many people. However, they were a stumbling block (as they were designed to be) for Catholics and Nonconformists, and for Quakers who would not swear any oath. See particularly E 157, C 185, C 193/9, C 213, C 214, C 215 and C 224 (sacrament certificates for 1673 to 1778), KB 22 (sacrament certificates 1676 to 1828), E 157, E 169 (oath rolls of jurors).

Places of worship

Registers of non-Anglican places of worship from 1689 to 1852 are in RG 31.

Plundered ministers

Plundered ministers were ministers with Parliamentary sympathies who had suffered losses at royalist hands. Records of yearly sums to be paid by 'delinquent' (that is, royalist) impropriators – who bought the right to tithes in return for paying the minister a salary – from 1644 to 1650 to named ministers who had suffered in the Civil War are in SP 22.

Protestation Oath

This oath from 1641–2 was to Protestantism in general and was intended to identify Catholics (though there is anecdotal evidence that some Catholics signed). This very important source (arranged by hundreds within counties) is in the House of Lords Record Office. However, returns for many counties are published and the National Archives is likely to have the published version.

See *The Protestation Returns 1641–42 and other contemporary listings*, Jeremy Gibson and Alan Dell (Federation of Family History Societies, 1995 and later editions).

Other listings for the same period include the Collection in aid of distressed Protestants in Ireland 1641–2 and various covenants and petitions addressed to Parliament.

Quakers (Society of Friends)

Authenticated registers of births, marriages, deaths and burials are in RG 6.

Quarter Sessions

Those who refused to attend church could be presented at Quarter Sessions. Before the Civil War those who had religious objections are almost certain to have been Catholics.

During the Civil War and Commonwealth period the Established Church did not exist, so the laws relating to compulsory attendance were in abeyance. From 1662 to 1689 there was a great deal of pressure on non-attenders – but the lists of those presented are sometimes not differentiated, so we often cannot tell which were Papists, Anabaptists, Sectaries or Quakers. No one was presented for non-attendance after 1689.

These records are not at the National Archives, but versions of many early ones are published and may be in the library.

See in particular *Middlesex County Records*, old series, vols. 1–4, 1549–1685 by J.C. Jeaffreson, who abstracted every reference relating to 'conventiclers' and recusants.

In general, see *Quarter Sessions Records for Family Historians*, Jeremy Gibson (Fedcration of Family History Societies, 1982 and later).

Recusant Rolls

These feature the names of Catholics who had been formally convicted between 1591 and 1691. They are in E 376 and 377.

Religious census 1851

This is chiefly concerned with the number of people who attended services on the chosen census day in 1851. It gives no general lists of the names of those attending, but can be useful for context. Records are in HO 129.

Return of papists' estates

From 1717 to 1778 the details of Catholic lands were supposed to be enrolled at Quarter Sessions; records are in E 174.

Russian Orthodox Church

Records of births, baptisms, marriages and deaths between 1721 and 1927 (also including the Greek Orthodox Church) are in RG 8/111–304.

Sacrament certificates

These had to be produced by people holding civil, military or naval office, or commissions from the Crown following the Test Acts of 1672 and 1673. Entries in the National Archives for the Westminster Courts only between 1673 and 1778 are in C 224; those between 1700 and 1827 are in E 196; those between 1676 and 1828 are in KB 22; and those for the Palatinate of Chester between 1673 and 1768 are in CHES 4. Other material may be in local Quarter Sessions records.

Superstitious uses

These relate to lands given to provide income for illegal Catholic purposes such as prayers for the dead, the support of priests or nuns, or the education of children abroad. Commissions of enquiry from 1552 to 1744 are in FEC 1; those from 1681 to 1699 are in C 295. Registers of estates given to superstitious uses in 1716 are in FEC 2/68–69, 120.

Wills and Letters of Administrations

Wills were proved, or letters giving the right to administer the deceased person's effects were issued, by the Bishop's Court in each diocese. Nowadays they are almost all in the appropriate county record office.

Most wills are not in the National Archives, but are likely to be in the appropriate county record office. See *Probate Jurisdictions: Where to look for wills* by Jeremy Gibson and Else Churchill (Federation of Family History Societies, 1980 and later editions).

The National Archives has the records of the Prerogative Court of Canterbury which dealt with a great many mainstream wills in London and the Home Counties, and the wills of those who had property in a number of lesser jurisdictions. These are now all online on the National Archives' website. They include the wills of many foreigners, not Anglican and possibly not Christian, but they used the same system as everyone else. See the PROB series.

Wills might be disputed before they were proved, and there are many records of this in the PROB series. Disputes often arose later as to whether the terms and conditions were carried out. Some were heard in ecclesiastical courts; others in Chancery or King's (Queen's)

Bench. In many cases disputes over the will were linked with other matters which appear in any of the equity courts.

None of the Nonconformist groups made any objection to using the Bishops' Courts for proving wills, nor did the court object to hearing them. Quakers had a certain amount of difficulty as regards swearing the oath to administer well and truly, but after a while they were allowed to affirm.

Between 1717 and 1778 Catholics were supposed to be enrolled on the Close Rolls so that the authorities could see who was inheriting their land. However, this did not happen very much in practice.

Letters of Administration were granted to administer the estates of those who had not left a will, or property not dealt with by the will. They were issued by the Bishops' Court until 1858, but otherwise there is no religious aspect. Nor is there a religious aspect to the Death Duty Registers in IR 26 and 27, also now online.

Useful addresses and websites

Addresses

Baptist Missionary Society, Regent's Park College, Pusey Street, Oxford, OX1 2LB, Tel: 01865 288142

British Library, 96 Euston Road, London, NW1 2DB, Tel: 020 7412 7332, Website: *www.bl.uk*

British Library Newspaper Collection, Colindale Avenue, London, NW9 5HE, Tel: 020 7412 7353, Email: newspaper@bl.uk, Website: *www.bl.uk/ collections/newspapers.html*

Catholic Central Library, St Michael's Abbey, Farnborough Road, Farnborough, Hants, GU14 7NQ, Tel: 01252 546105

Catholic Record Society, 12 Melbourne Place, Wolsingham, County Durham, DL13 3EH, Tel: 01388 527747, Website: *www.catholic-history.org.uk/crs*

Church Mission Society, Partnership House, 157 Waterloo Road, London, SE1 8UU, Tel: 020 7928 8681, Website: *www.cms-uk.org*

Church of Jesus Christ of Latter-day Saints, 185 Penns Lane, Sutton Coldfield, West Midlands, B76 1JU, Tel: 0121 384 2028, Website: *www.familysearch.org*

Commonwealth War Graves Commission,
2 Marlow Road, Maidenhead, Berkshire, SL6 7DX,
Tel: 01628 634221, Website: *www.cwgc.org*

Diocesan Record Offices, For localities consult J.
Gibson, *Bishops' Transcripts and Marriage Licences,
Bonds and Allegations*, 5th edn (Federation of Family
History Societies, 2001) – then see CRO above

Dr Williams's Library, 14 Gordon Square, London,
WC1H 0AR, Tel: 0207 387 3727,
Email: *enquiries@dwlib.co.uk,*
Website: *www.dwlib.co.uk*

Family Records Centre, 1 Myddelton Street,
London, EC1R 1UW, Tel: 0208 392 5300,
Email: *frc@nationalarchives.gov.uk,*
Website: *www.familyrecords.gov.uk/frc*

Federation of Family History Societies, Administrator,
PO Box 2425, Coventry, CV5 6YX, Tel: 07041 492032,
Website: *www.ffhs.org.uk*

Genealogical Society of Utah, British Isles Family
History Service Centre, 185 Penns Lane, Sutton
Coldfield, Birmingham, West Midlands, B76 1JU

General Register Office, Certificate Services Section,
PO Box 2, Southport, PR8 2JD, Tel: 0845 603 7788,
Email: *certificate.services@gro.gsi.gov.uk,*
Website: *www.gro.gov.uk*

General Register Office for Scotland, New Register
House, Edinburgh, EH1 3YT, Tel: 0131 314 4433,
Email: *records@gro-scotland.gov.uk,*
Website: *www.gro-scotland.gov.uk*

Guildhall Library, Aldermanbury, London, EC2P 2EJ,
Tel: 020 7332 1868/1870, Website: *www.
cityoflondon.gov.uk/corporation/leisure_heritage/*

Huguenot Society of Great Britain and Ireland, The
Huguenot Library, University College, Gower Street,
London, WC1E 6BT, Tel: 020 7679 5199,
Email: *secretary@huguenotsociety.org.uk*,
Website: *www.huguenotsociety.org.uk* or *www.ucl.
ac.uk/library/huguenot*

Institute of Historical Research, University of London,
Senate House, Malet Street, London, WC1E 7HU,
Tel: 020 7862 8740, Website: *www.history.ac.uk*

Lambeth Palace Library, London, SE1 7JU,
Tel: 020 7928 6222,
Website: *www.lambethpalacelibrary.org*

The National Archives, Kew, Richmond, Surrey,
TW9 4DU, Tel: 020 8876 3444,
Website: *www.nationalarchives.gov.uk*

National Library of Wales, Aberystwyth, Ceredigion,
Wales, SY23 3BU, Tel: 01970 632 800,

Office for National Statistics
Certificate Enquiries, PO Box 2, Southport, Merseyside,
PR8 2JD, Tel: 0845 603 7788,
Website: *www.gro.gov.uk/gro/content/certificates*

Religious Society of Friends (Quakers), Friends'
House, 173–177 Euston Road, London, NW1 2BJ,
Tel: 020 7663 1135, Website: *www.quaker.org.uk*

Society of Genealogists, 14 Charterhouse Buildings,
Goswell Road, London, EC1M 7BA,
Tel: 020 7251 8799, Email: *library@sog.org.uk*,
Website: *www.sog.org.uk*

Websites

www.a2s.org.uk The Access to Archives database
contains catalogues describing nearly 8 million items,
dating from the 900s to the present day.

www.ancestry.co.uk An invaluable resource to genealogists researching the United Kingdom and Ireland.

www.archon.nationalarchives.gov.uk A list of UK repositories with contact details and website links.

www.asht.info The website of the Anglo Sikh Heritage Trail.

www.bl.uk The website of the British Library.

www.casbah.ac.uk The website of the Caribbean Studies and the history of Black and Asian peoples in the UK

www.catholic-history.org.uk/crs The website of the Catholic Record Society.

www.cms-uk.org The website of the Church Mission Society.

www.dwlib.co.uk The website of Dr Williams's Library.

www.familyhistoryonline.net Pay-for-view access to a series of databases collected by the Federation of Family History Societies, especially to census and parish register indexes. Free access to 1881 census surname index.

www.familyrecords.gov.uk A 'portal' site with links to official sites for UK family history research.

www.familysearch.org The Church of Latter-day Saints website, including access to the International Genealogical Index (IGI).

www.ffhs.org.uk The website of the Federation of Family History Societies.

www.genuki.org.uk A comprehensive 'virtual reference library' of particular relevance to the UK and Ireland.

www.gro.gov.uk/gro/content/certificates The website of the Office for National Statistics.

www.history.ac.uk The website of the Institute of Historical Research.

www.huguenotsociety.org.uk The website of the Huguenot Society of Great Britain and Ireland.

www.lambethpalacelibrary.org The website of Lambeth Palace Library.

www.leics.gov.uk/museums/records/index.htm The website of the record office for Leicestershire.

www.llgc.org.uk The website of the National Library of Wales.

www.movinghere.org.uk The Moving Here website.

www.nationalarchives.gov.uk The website of The National Archives, with access to the online catalogue and much more.

www.ochs.org.uk/research/hindu_archive.html The website of the Oxford Centre for Hindu Studies.

www.oxcis.ac.uk The website of the Oxford Centre for Islamic Studies.

www.quaker.org.uk The website of the Religious Society of Friends (Quakers).

www.salidaa.org.uk/salidaa/site/Home The website of the South Asian Diaspora Literature and Arts Archive.

www.s-asian.cam.ac.uk The website of the Centre of South Asian Studies, University of Cambridge.

www.scotlandspeople.gov.uk An indispensable resource for Scottish family history, providing access to Scottish civil registration records, parish registers, census returns and wills.

www.sog.org.uk The website of the Society of Genealogists.

Further reading

General reading

A. Adolph, *Tracing your Family History* (Collins, 2004)

D. Annal, *Easy Family History* (The National Archives, 2005)

A. Bevan, *Tracing Your Ancestors in the National Archives*, 7th edn (The National Archives, 2006)

J. Cole and J. Titford, *Tracing Your Family Tree* (Countryside Books, 2004)

S. Colwell, *Dictionary of Genealogical Sources in the Public Record Office* (Weidenfeld and Nicolson, 1992)

M. Herber, *Ancestral Trails* (Sutton, 2004)

D. Hey, *Journeys in Family History* (The National Archives, 2004)

R. Kershaw and M. Pearsall, *Family History on the Move* (The National Archives, 2006)

M. Pearsall, *Family History Companion* (The National Archives, 2007)

Reader's Digest, *Explore Your Family's Past* (Reader's Digest, 2000)

W. Spencer, *Family History in the Wars* (The National Archives, 2007)

Other topics

J. Besse, *Sufferings of the People Called Quakers for*

the Testimony of a Good Conscience (1752); reprinted as Sufferings of the Early Quakers: Yorkshire (1998); North England (2000); America and the West Indies (2001); London and Middlesex (2002); Ireland, Scotland and Wales (2003); South West England (2004); Southern England (2006); East Anglia and East Midlands (in preparation for 2008) (Sessions of York)

Geoffrey R. Breed, My Ancestors were Baptists (Society of Genealogists, 1995)

D. Clifford, My Ancestors were Congregationalists (Society of Genealogists, 1997)

M. Gandy, English Nonconformity for Family Historians (Federation of Family History Societies, 1998)

M. Gandy, Tracing Catholic Ancestry (Federation of Family History Societies, 1998)

L. Gibbens, Using Death and Burial Records for Family Historians (Federation of Family History Societies, 1997)

J. Gibson, Bishops' Transcripts and Marriage Licences, Bonds and Allegations (Federation of Family History Societies, 4th edn, 1997)

J. Gibson, The Hearth Tax and other Stuart tax lists and the Association Oath Rolls (Federation of Family History Societies, 1985 and later edns)

J. Gibson, Quarter Sessions Records for Family Historians (Federation of Family History Societies, 1982 and later)

J. Gibson, Tudor and Stuart Tax Lists (Federation of Family History Societies, 1985)

J. Gibson and E. Churchill, Probate Jurisdictions: Where to look for wills (Federation of Family History Societies, 1980 and later edns)

J. Gibson and A. Dell, The Protestation Returns 1641–42

and other contemporary listings (Federation of Family History Societies, 1995 and later edns)

J. Gibson and C. Rogers, *Coroners' Records in England and Wales* (Federation of Family History Societies, 1997)

G. Hodgett, 'The State of the Ex-Religious and Former Chantry Priests in the Diocese of Lincoln 1547–1574' (Lincoln Record Society, vol. 53, 1959)

R. Jensen and M. Thorp (eds), *Mormons in Early Victorian Britain* (University of Utah Press, 1989)

A. Lawes, 'The Dissolution of the Monasteries and Chantries: Sources in the National Archives' (*Genealogists' Magazine*, vol. 27, no. 11, September 2003)

W. Leary, *My Ancestors were Methodists* (Society of Genealogists, 1999)

C. L'Estrange Ewen, *Witch Hunting and Witch Trials* (Kegan Paul, Trench Trubner and Co., 1929)

P. Litton, *Using Baptism Records for Family Historians* (Federation of Family History Societies, 1996)

P. Litton, *Using Marriage Records for Family Historians* (Federation of Family History Societies, 1996)

E. Milligan and M. Thomas, *My Ancestors were Quakers* (Society of Genealogists, 1983)

M. Mullett, *Sources for the History of English Nonconformity 1660–1830* (British Records Association, 1991)

A. Ruston, *My Ancestors were English Presbyterians/Unitarians* (Society of Genealogists, 1993)

W. Shaw, *Letters of Denization and Acts of Naturalization 1603–1700* (Huguenot Society, vol. 18, 1911)

D. Steel, *National Index of Parish Registers*, vol. II (Society of Genealogists, 1973)

N.P. Tanner (ed.), *Kent Heresy Proceedings 1511–12* (Kent Archaeological Society, vol. 26, 1997)

N. Tanner (ed.), *Norwich Heresy Trials 1428–1431* (Camden Fourth Series, 1977)

P. Towey, *My Ancestor was a Clergyman* (Society of Genealogists, 2006)

H. Trevor-Roper, *The European Witchcraft Craze* (Penguin Books, 1967)

C. Tucker, *My Ancestors were Jewish* (Society of Genealogists, 2005)

S. Vertovec, *The Hindu Diaspora: Comparative Patterns* (Routledge, 2000)

P.K. Virdi, *The Grounds for Divorce in Hindu and English Law* (Motilal Banarsidass, 1972)

I. Waller, 'The Young and Tender Transplanted to Strengthen: Mormon emigrants from the British Isles' (*Genealogists' Magazine*, vol. 28, no. 12, December 2006)

R. Wiggins, *My Ancestors were in the Salvation Army* (Society of Genealogists, 1997)

J. Williams, 'Sources for Recusants in English Official Archives' (*Recusant History*, vol. 16, no. 4, Catholic Record Society, 1983)

See also various publications of the Catholic Family History Society, Catholic Record Society and Huguenot Society.

Index